Hedge Funds and Systemic Risk

Lloyd Dixon, Noreen Clancy, Krishna B. Kumar

The research described in this report was supported by a contribution by Christopher D. Petitt, principal of Blue Haystack, a financial research and consulting firm, and by the RAND Center for Corporate Ethics and Governance.

Library of Congress Control Number: 2012948078

ISBN 978-0-8330-7684-7

Published 2012 by the RAND Corporation
1776 Main Street, P.O. Box 2138, Santa Monica, CA 90407-2138
1200 South Hayes Street, Arlington, VA 22202-5050
4570 Fifth Avenue, Suite 600, Pittsburgh, PA 15213-2665
RAND URL: http://www.rand.org/
To order RAND documents or to obtain additional information, contact
Distribution Services: Telephone: (310) 451-7002;
Fax: (310) 451-6915; Email: order@rand.org

Preface

Hedge funds are investment pools open to high-net-worth investors and institutions but not to the general public. In part because of this restriction, hedge funds have, until recently, been subject to reduced reporting and oversight regulations. They have also been reluctant to provide even general information on their operations and strategies to the public, fearing that such information could be construed as making a public offering. The result has been very poor public understanding of hedge funds and their role in the financial system.

Like other participants in the financial system, hedge funds invested in many of the financial instruments linked to the financial crisis of 2007–2008. As a consequence, their role in the financial crisis and potential contribution to systemic risk have drawn increased attention from Congress, regulators, participants in the financial system, and researchers. With the passage of the Dodd-Frank Wall Street Reform and Consumer Protection Act of 2010 (Pub. L. 111-203), regulations are currently being developed that have the potential to significantly affect the hedge fund industry and its role in the financial system.

To improve the general understanding of hedge funds, this report provides an overview of the hedge fund industry, of hedge fund strategies and operations, and of the role of hedge funds in the financial system. To better understand how hedge funds might contribute to systemic risk, it investigates the role hedge funds played in the financial crisis and revisits the consequences of a large hedge fund's failure in the late 1990s. It also examines whether and how the ongoing financial reforms address the potential systemic risks posed by hedge funds.

This research was supported by a contribution by Christopher D. Petitt, principal of Blue Haystack, a financial research and consulting firm. It was also supported by the RAND Center for Corporate Ethics and Governance. The report should be of interest to policymakers, regulators, members of the financial community, and others interested in improving the stability of the U.S. financial system while maintaining its dynamism and efficiency.

The RAND Center for Corporate Ethics and Governance

The RAND Center for Corporate Ethics and Governance is committed to improving public understanding of corporate ethics, law, and governance and to identifying specific ways in which businesses can operate ethically, legally, and profitably. The center's work is supported by voluntary contributions from private-sector organizations and individuals with interests in research on these topics.

For more information on the RAND Center for Corporate Ethics and Governance, see http://lbr.rand.org/cceg or contact the director:

Michael Greenberg
Director, RAND Center for Corporate Ethics and Governance
4570 Fifth Avenue, Suite 600
Pittsburgh, PA 15213
412-683-2300 x4648
Michael_Greenberg@rand.org

Questions or comments about the monograph should be sent to the project lead:

Lloyd Dixon, Senior Economist
RAND Corporation
1776 Main Street, P.O. Box 2138
Santa Monica, CA 90407-2138
310-393-0411 x7480
Lloyd_Dixon@rand.org

Contents

Figures

Tables

Summary

Hedge funds are a dynamic part of the global financial system. Their managers engage in innovative investment strategies that can improve the performance of financial markets and facilitate the flow of capital from savers to users. Although hedge funds play a useful role in the financial system, there is concern that they can contribute to financial instability. The collapse of Long-Term Capital Management (LTCM) in 1998 raised awareness that hedge funds could be a source of risk to the financial system. Hedge funds also invested heavily in many of the financial instruments at the heart of the financial crisis of 2007–2008, and it is appropriate to ask whether they contributed to the crisis.

This report explores the extent to which hedge funds create or contribute to systemic risk. By *systemic risk*, we mean the risk of a major and rapid disruption in one or more of the core functions of the financial system caused by the initial failure of one or more financial firms or a segment of the financial system. To do this, we explore the role hedge funds played in the financial crisis. We also examine the consequences of the 1998 failure of LTCM, a large hedge fund. In addition, we examine whether and how the recent financial-reform legislation, the Dodd-Frank Wall Street Reform and Consumer Protection Act of 2010, addresses the potential systemic risks posed by hedge funds.

The analysis is based on review of relevant literature; interviews with 45 people, including hedge fund managers, hedge fund lawyers, investors, regulators, staff of industry associations, congressional staff, researchers, and policy analysts; and analysis of data provided by a leading firm that compiles statistics on hedge fund operations and performance.

Overview of the Hedge Fund Industry

Generally speaking, hedge funds are investment pools that can solicit funds from large institutions and wealthy investors but not from the general public. As a result, they face fewer restrictions than funds that are marketed to the general public, such as mutual funds. Unlike mutual funds, hedge funds can use leverage without limit, can engage in short sales,[1] can impose restrictions on investor withdrawals, are free to pursue any investment strategy they choose, and are exempt from many reporting and other regulatory oversight requirements. Salient characteristics of the industry follow:

- The investor assets managed by the hedge fund industry (assets under management, or AUM) have grown rapidly in the past 15 years but are still not large compared with mutual funds (one-tenth as large) or banks (one-sixth as large). Hedge funds do, however, account for a substantial share of the trading volume in many markets.
- The sources of hedge fund capital are diverse, with a least one-third coming from pension funds, endowments, and foundations. Hedge fund returns thus do not benefit just wealthy individuals but individuals across the economic spectrum.
- A sizable proportion of the AUM industry-wide is invested in a relatively small percentage of funds: More than 70 percent of AUM is invested in less than 10 percent of the approximately

---

[1]   A short seller essentially sells a security first and buys it back later. Long investors do the reverse.

10,000 funds worldwide.[2] That said, the industry is not considered concentrated according to standard measures of industry concentration.

- Even though short sales are a central part of many hedge fund investment strategies, hedge funds take both long and short positions. In fact, a much higher percentage of AUM is in funds that invest only long or have a long bias than in funds with a short bias.

Hedge funds can, in principle, contribute to systemic risk through a credit channel and a market channel. Systemic risk can arise through the credit channel when hedge fund losses result in default to creditors and the financial institutions with which they do business and these losses go on to cause broader problems in the financial system. Systemic risk through the market channel can arise when hedge funds drive unsustainable increases in asset prices during financial booms or contribute to price declines that overshoot long-run market equilibrium in financial crises.

Hedge Fund Contributions to the Financial Crisis

Our assessment is that hedge funds were not a primary cause of the financial crisis, although some aspects of their operations contributed to the crisis. The roles played by credit-rating agencies, mortgage lenders, and inadequately backed credit default swaps (CDSs) were far more important. In this section, we summarize our findings on hedge fund contributions through the credit and market channels.

Contributions to the Financial Crisis Through the Credit Channel

Hedge funds suffered substantial losses during the financial crisis, and approximately 18 percent of funds (in number) were liquidated in 2008.[3] However, there is little indication that hedge fund losses led

---

[2] Data provided to the authors by eVestment|HFN.

[3] Data provided to the authors by eVestment|HFN.

to significant losses at prime brokers and other creditors.[4] It appears that prime brokers and other hedge fund creditors required adequate margin and collateral to protect themselves against hedge fund losses.

Contributions to the Financial Crisis Through the Market Channel
Buildup of the Housing Bubble
Hedge funds were on both sides of the subprime-mortgage market. On the one hand, hedge funds invested in the mortgage-backed securities (MBSs) and collateralized debt obligations (CDOs) that contributed to the buildup of the housing bubble. Conversely, by shorting subprime mortgages and banks that were heavily exposed to subprime debt, hedge funds called attention to the growing bubble. They also provided funds to this market at the trough of the crash, possibly limiting further declines. In light of these opposing factors, no strong case can be made that hedge funds were a significant contributor to the financial crisis through the buildup of the housing bubble. Other factors, such as the behavior of credit-rating agencies, the availability of inadequately backed CDSs, and careless lending practices appear to be far more important.

Hedge Fund Deleveraging
In reaction to substantial losses in MBSs, Wall Street banks began to reduce the credit available to some highly leveraged hedge funds in the summer of 2008. At the same time, hedge funds faced unprecedented withdrawals by their investors. These forces created pressures on hedge funds to sell assets during the peak of the financial crisis, potentially contributing to the rapid decline in asset prices. Rapid declines in asset prices can create self-reinforcing cycles of margin calls, additional asset liquidations, and further price declines.

The pernicious effects of deleveraging are magnified by lack of liquidity and leverage. The evaporation of liquidity in many markets during the financial crisis caught many hedge fund managers by surprise and demonstrates how assumptions about liquidity can quickly

---

[4]   A prime broker is an institution (or part of an institution) that offers various settlement, custody, and financing services to hedge funds and other specialized investment or dealing operations.

break down. Data are not available, however, to determine the extent to which hedge funds were forced to sell in illiquid markets, further deepening the financial crisis.

Even though some hedge funds are highly leveraged, hedge fund leverage does not stand out as a central contributor to the financial crisis. Hedge fund leverage started to decrease prior to the first signs of the financial crisis in mid-2007, even as the leverage of investment banks, commercial banks, and the financial sector as a whole continued to increase. At the peak of the crisis in late 2008, investment banks had the highest leverage.

No strong conclusions can be made about the extent to which hedge fund deleveraging contributed to the financial crisis. There is evidence that hedge funds contributed to downward price pressure and withdrew liquidity in some markets, but it is hard to assess whether the effects were substantial. What is more, investor inflows into funds that invest primarily in mortgage-related securities suggest that hedge funds also injected liquidity into some markets.

Short Selling

Short selling is a central part of many hedge fund investment strategies, and hedge fund shorting has been blamed for contributing to the financial crisis. The U.S. Securities and Exchange Commission's (SEC's) ban on shorting financial stocks between September 19 and October 8, 2008, indicates that at least some in government were concerned about the impact of short selling. Although some studies identify short selling as a significant contributor to the financial crisis, the bulk of research does not conclude that short selling played a major role. The banks' financial problems were much more directly related to their exposure to toxic mortgage assets and investor realization of the extent of this exposure than to the short selling of their stocks by hedge funds.

Hedge Fund Runs on Prime Brokers

During 2008, hedge fund managers withdrew tens of billions of dollars in assets from prime brokers and their parent investment banks. These withdrawals were essentially a run on the bank, analogous to bank runs by individual depositors during the Great Depression, and contributed to the financial crisis. Even though hedge fund withdrawals arguably weakened some prime brokers and their parent organizations, there were valid reasons for the withdrawals. Hedge funds were concerned that their assets could be frozen if the banks that held them declared bankruptcy. Such a worst-case scenario did indeed occur in the September 2008 bankruptcy of Lehman Brothers Holdings.

Potential Contributions to Systemic Risk and Regulatory Responses

Although hedge funds did not play a pivotal role in the financial crisis, examination of the crisis reveals ways in which they can potentially contribute to systemic risk. Similarly, review of the LTCM episode illuminates potential threats to financial-system stability. From our analysis, we identify six areas of concern regarding hedge funds' potential contribution to systemic risk:

- lack of information on hedge funds
- lack of appropriate margin in derivatives trades
- runs on prime brokers
- short selling
- compromised risk-management incentives
- lack of portfolio liquidity and excessive leverage.

We also examine the extent to which Dodd-Frank and other recent regulations allay these concerns.

Lack of Information on Hedge Funds

Following the LTCM collapse and during the financial crisis, regulators complained about the lack of transparency in hedge fund positions, leverage, and asset valuation and were frustrated by their inability to collect data on hedge funds. Without such information, it is not possible to identify building systemic risk in the hedge fund industry.

Dodd-Frank aggressively addresses gaps in the information available to regulators on hedge fund operations, investment strategies, and investment positions.[5] The legislation will also result in far more information being available on derivatives trades, trades that were at the heart of the financial crisis, and short sales. Although these provisions are far reaching, limitations on the new information requirements remain. Foreign hedge fund advisers are exempt, which could make it difficult to assess the overall systemic risk posed by hedge funds. Many foreign jurisdictions are imposing reporting requirements similar to those in the United States, and the resulting information may improve understanding about the systemic risk posed by hedge funds globally as long as the information is comparable and shared among regulators.

Although the new information on hedge funds may be of substantial value to systemic-risk regulators, it comes at a cost. Those we interviewed believed that complying with the reporting requirements would be costly, although the demands on smaller firms are much less than on larger firms. The reporting requirements thus do not appear to create significant entry barriers. Industry participants with whom we spoke are also concerned that information provided to regulators might be publicly released, revealing the secrets of their strategies. Failure to protect sensitive information can reduce the incentives for funds to enter or remain in the business, limiting the benefits that they provide to the financial system.

Lack of Appropriate Margin in Derivatives Trades

The LTCM experience illustrates the importance of imposing appropriate margin requirements on derivatives trades. Had the derivatives trades been centrally cleared by an organization that enforced appropriate margin requirements, the LTCM debacle might never have occurred. Increased market discipline following LTCM's failure

---

[5] We use *address* to mean that an effort is being made to tackle or solve a problem. We do not use it to signal that the problem has been fixed or even lessened by the regulatory reform.

appears to have resulted in more-sensible margin requirements, but, absent regulation, the possibility remains that counterparties might once again become lax in the imposition of margin requirements.

Dodd-Frank overhauls the derivatives market, giving regulators the authority to impose margin and other requirements that will cover the risk of default. Absent the exemptions of major categories of derivatives in the rulemaking process, the reforms should help prevent the buildup of highly leveraged positions that can lead to the rapid failure of a large fund.

Runs on Prime Brokers

Hedge fund runs on investment banks were a contributing factor in the financial crisis, illustrating the vulnerability of prime brokers to withdrawals by their hedge fund customers and the importance of maintaining sufficient cash and liquid assets to weather them. One might argue that the solution is for banks to maintain strong balance sheets, but economic modeling has shown how banks can be subject to runs even if many depositors know that negative information about the bank is inaccurate. There is thus a public interest in reducing incentives for hedge funds to withdraw assets from prime brokers at the first hint of trouble. The crisis demonstrates the importance of segregating hedge fund assets from assets of the prime broker's parent organization. Without such segregation, even a remote possibility of insolvency can lead to hedge fund withdrawals, increasing the probability of insolvency in a self-reinforcing cycle.

The reforms go a long way in addressing factors that can lead to hedge fund runs on prime brokers. Dodd-Frank contains provisions that protect the margin that hedge funds post with prime brokers on their derivatives positions. A prime broker must segregate these assets from its own account for certain types of swaps and give a party the option of segregating the assets for others. These new provisions should reduce the incentives for hedge funds to withdraw funds from their prime brokers at the first sign of trouble. However, the hedge funds will still have the option to deposit funds in nonsegregated accounts at foreign subsidiaries of U.S. banks. The potential remains that hedge fund runs at these subsidiaries will weaken the parent organization.

Short Selling

Although there is little evidence that short selling by hedge funds was a significant contributor to the financial crisis, some academic researchers and industry participants remain concerned about opportunistic short selling. Concern remains that short selling by a large hedge fund or multiple hedge funds can result in an unjustified fall in stock prices or can cause a decline in the real value of the firm. The decline might be so rapid that there is no opportunity for the firm to dispel rumors about its financial health or for investors to provide additional capital before the firm collapses. Such collapses can pose a risk to the financial system and reduce the level of economic activity.

Shortly before the financial crisis, the SEC rescinded a rule that had restricted short selling in a declining market. The so-called *uptick rule* had been in place since 1937.[6] Following the financial crisis, the SEC reinstated a modified version of the rule. The modified approach contains a circuit breaker that is tripped if a stock price declines by 10 percent or more and a modified uptick rule that remains in place for one to two days.[7] The SEC has also strengthened prohibitions against naked short selling and is implementing provisions in Dodd-Frank that require public disclosure of short sales by securities on a monthly basis.[8]

The new restrictions on short sales limit a short seller's ability to push down prices in a declining market. However, it remains to be seen whether the 10-percent trigger and modified uptick rule are stringent enough to make much of a difference. For example, a 10-percent trigger would not have stopped what some analysts consider to be a bear raid on Citigroup in the fall of 2007. Public disclosure of short sales might make it easier to detect and deter opportunistic short selling; however, public disclosure may make hedge funds less likely to engage in short selling and reduce the benefits that they can provide to investors and financial markets. Careful analysis of the costs and benefits of the new regulations on short sales is warranted.

---

[6] SEC, 2012, p. 15.

[7] SEC, 2012, p. 56.

[8] In a naked short sale, the short seller agrees to sell a stock without first borrowing it.

Compromised Risk-Management Incentives

The failure of the Bear Stearns Companies hedge funds in the period leading up to the financial crisis caused substantial losses to the parent investment bank, which was subsequently taken over by Morgan Stanley with the help of federal regulators. This sequence of events raises concerns about embedding hedge funds within larger financial institutions. In the case of Bear Stearns, reputational concerns led it to bail out the hedge funds, creating additional strain on a systemically important institution. The Bear Stearns experience more generally underscores the dangers of hedge funds that are directly or indirectly subsidized by taxpayers. Such subsidies might be due to the parent organization's access to the Federal Reserve discount window and can result if regulators rescue a fund or if a parent organization is deemed too big to fail. In such situations, hedge fund managers no longer bear the full consequences of their investment decisions, and inadequate risk management can result in the buildup of systemic risk.

Dodd-Frank limits bank investments in hedge funds (the part of the act that is referred to as the Volcker Rule). The restrictions are significant: We estimate that JPMorgan Chase, the largest U.S. bank by asset size, would be able to invest only $3.24 billion in hedge funds, far less than the $26 billion in AUM that was managed by JPMorgan Chase hedge funds in 2011. By limiting the stakes that banks can hold in hedge funds, Dodd-Frank addresses one way in which hedge fund managers may not bear the full cost of risk taking. Banks will be limited in how much taxpayer-subsidized capital they can invest in hedge funds, and hedge fund managers may think it less likely that they would be bailed out by taxpayer-subsidized banks.

Lack of Portfolio Liquidity and Excessive Leverage

Although it is difficult to come to strong conclusions about the extent to which hedge fund deleveraging contributed to the financial crisis, the potential remains for hedge fund deleveraging to cause weakness in the financial system.

High leverage does not appear currently to be a problem across the hedge fund industry, but that does not mean that it cannot increase rapidly in the future. Perhaps of greater concern than high leverage is the potential for decreased liquidity of hedge fund investments. The financial crisis caused both hedge fund managers and investors to reassess assumptions made about the liquidity of their investments. Recent academic research suggests that it is increasingly important to pay attention to the liquidity of hedge fund investments, and regulators should realize that, even if no one hedge fund may be large enough to pose a systemic risk to the financial system, negative shocks can cause hedge funds as a group to unwind their positions at the same time, with ramifications cascading through the economy. Thus, it may not be enough to pay attention to only the largest hedge funds when considering systemic risk. The consequence for regulators is that the financial condition of the entire hedge fund industry, not just of the largest funds, is relevant.

Prior to Dodd-Frank, there was no direct regulation of hedge fund leverage and liquidity. Rather, control of leverage and liquidity relied on market discipline and indirect regulation through banks and prime brokers that were, in turn, overseen by regulators. The LTCM experience demonstrates that the oversight of hedge funds by prime brokers and other counterparties can break down, while the track record in the ensuing years illustrates that this type of indirect regulation can work. However, there is no guarantee that market discipline and indirect regulation will remain strong. Once memory of LTCM and the financial crisis recedes, oversight by prime brokers and other creditors might weaken.

Dodd-Frank provides a framework for financial regulators to directly regulate hedge fund investment practices that contribute to systemic risk, including the establishment of leverage and liquidity requirements. Regulators have recently adopted criteria that will be used to designate hedge funds as systemically important nonbank financial companies (SINBFCs), which would then be regulated by the Federal Reserve Bank. It remains to be seen how many hedge funds will be so designated, but initial indications are that the number will be small or modest. Not many funds exceed the $50 billion in total assets[9]

---

[9] In contrast to the AUM measure used earlier to characterize the size of hedge funds, *total assets* reflects the overall positions of the fund. As a first approximation, it equals investor

that will be used in the first step in the screening process, and funds that pass the first screen may subsequently be dropped from consideration in later stages of the multistage designation process.[10]

It may well be appropriate that very few hedge funds be designated as SINBFCs. Indeed, a reasonable regulatory strategy is to induce large hedge funds to reduce their size so that they are not considered systemically important. However, two observations are worth making. First, the designation of only a small number of SINBFCs means that the oversight of hedge funds will rely on market discipline and indirect regulation. Market discipline can erode, and it is difficult to see how prime brokers could effectively monitor systemic risk in some dimensions. For example, a prime broker does not appear particularly well equipped to monitor the liquidity risks posed across the hedge fund industry because it is common practice for one hedge fund to use multiple prime brokers. Second, a firm-by-firm designation process does not address the risk of a large number of medium-sized firms following similar investment strategies. Dodd-Frank gives financial regulators a great deal of discretion in crafting regulations, so regulations could, in principle, be tailored to address industry-wide liquidity issues. However, there is no guarantee that such risks will be addressed.

Position limits authorized by the act can also reduce concentration and, in principle, increase the liquidity of hedge fund portfolios. There are reasons, however, that the effectiveness of position limits may be compromised. First, the U.S. Commodity Futures Trading Commission (CFTC) has a great deal of discretion in implementing these regulations, so their effectiveness will become apparent only over time. Second, the limits apply only to physical commodities, so they will not be able to address the illiquidity that can be created by large positions in markets for financial derivatives. Third, position limits may not be well suited to the systemic risks that result when large numbers of medium-sized hedge funds take similar positions. Finally, positions that are required for bona fide hedging are excluded from limit calculations. Although such an exemption is sensible, difficulty in determin-

---

equity multiplied by fund leverage.

[10] FSOC, 2012.

ing when positions are for bona fide hedging and when they are not may compromise the efficacy of position limits.

In sum, it is not clear that the financial reforms will do much to change potential behaviors of hedge funds in terms of leverage and portfolio liquidity. First, although regulators will have a great deal more information about hedge fund strategies and positions, it might be unrealistic to expect regulators to effectively use it to reduce systemic risk. The time delays in reporting may be too great, and the hedge fund industry may move far too fast for regulators to have any impact. For example, would the regulatory apparatus be nimble enough to detect the rapid buildup of highly leveraged bets that occurred at LTCM? Second, few, if any, hedge funds will be subject to direct regulation under the new regime, leaving the oversight of hedge fund leverage and liquidity to prime brokers that are, in turn, overseen by the Federal Reserve. Such oversight may not result in any meaningful restraint, particularly as memories of the financial crisis fade. The potential thus remains for the buildup of highly leveraged, illiquid hedge fund portfolios and massive deleveraging when prime brokers or investors withdraw credit and capital in response to a financial shock.

Conclusions

From our analysis, we conclude that hedge funds can contribute to systemic risk. Although they were not a primary cause of the financial crisis, some aspects of their operations contributed to the crisis. The collapse of LTCM also illustrates the risks they can pose to the stability of the financial system. Dodd-Frank and other reforms are addressing many aspects of hedge fund operations that can create systemic risk. The reforms appear to aggressively address the first three areas of concern identified in this summary (lack of information on hedge funds, lack of appropriate margin in derivatives trades, and runs on prime brokers). They make considerable progress in addressing the next two (short selling and compromised risk management incentives), although questions remain about the effectiveness and comprehensiveness of the approach. The concern least well addressed is the potential lack of port-folio liquidity and excessive leverage.

Looking forward, policymakers and regulators should care-fully monitor hedge fund leverage and collect data on and monitor the liquidity of hedge fund portfolios. They not only should focus on the largest funds but should also pay attention to risk posed by the large number of small or medium-sized funds pursuing similar strat-egies. Finally, they should be on the lookout for important classes of derivatives that trade outside Dodd-Frank's regulatory structure and should continue to pursue coordination of regulations across national jurisdictions.

Hedge funds need not be the primary concern of regulators as they work to improve the stability of the world's financial system. However, policymakers should strive to better understand and monitor the systemic risks posed by this part of the financial system. And they should weigh any reduction in systemic risk due to increased regula-tion against the reduction in the hedge funds' ability to provide value to their investors and the economy more generally, as well as the costs of overseeing numerous medium-sized financial institutions.

Acknowledgments

This project would not have been possible without significant contributions by many people. First, we would like to thank Chris Petitt of Blue Haystack for the many hours he spent with us discussing the workings of the hedge fund industry and the issues that the financial system faces more generally and for feedback on report outlines and drafts. We would also like to thank the many people we interviewed during the course of the project. The interviews were done on a confidential basis, so we cannot thank them by name, but we benefited from their deep knowledge of the subject area. We are also indebted to Peter Laurelli of eVestment|HFN for working with us to determine what data his organization could provide for the study and for taking the time to explain and interpret them.

Very constructive peer reviews were provided by Eric Helland at RAND and Claremont McKenna College and Nicole M. Boyson at Northeastern University. We also received valuable comments from Stuart J. Kaswell and Benjamin Allensworth at the Managed Funds Association, from Paul N. Roth of Schulte Roth and Zabel, and from the SEC Division of Investment Management. We thank them for the time and thought that they put into their comments.

Among our RAND colleagues, we thank James N. Dertouzos, former director of RAND Law, Business, and Regulation, and Michael D. Greenberg, director of the RAND Center for Corporate Ethics and Governance, for guidance during the course of the project. Julie Kim, a senior engineer at RAND, linked potential sponsors with interested research staff and provided feedback throughout the project.

Susan M. Gates, director of the quality-assurance process for the project, provided helpful comments on the draft and reviewer responses, as did Paul Heaton, director of the RAND Institute for Civil Justice. Lisa Bernard provided skillful editing, and Jamie Morikawa, director of strategic partnerships for the RAND Institute for Civil Justice, helped secure funding for the study, skillfully coordinated the relationships with project sponsors, and facilitated contacts with practitioners.

Abbreviations

AIG	American International Group
AIMA	Alternative Investment Management Association
AUM	assets under management
CDO	collateralized debt obligation
CDS	credit default swap
CEO	chief executive officer
CFTC	U.S. Commodity Futures Trading Commission
DOJ	U.S. Department of Justice
FCIC	Financial Crisis Inquiry Commission
FDIC	Federal Deposit Insurance Corporation
FINRA	Financial Industry Regulatory Authority
FOF	fund of funds
FOMC	Federal Open Market Committee
FSA	Financial Services Authority
FSOC	Financial Stability Oversight Council
FTC	Federal Trade Commission

GAO	U.S. Government Accountability Office (before July 7, 2004, the U.S. General Accounting Office)
HHI	Herfindahl-Hirschman index
IMF	International Monetary Fund
JOBS	Jumpstart Our Business Startups
LTCM	Long-Term Capital Management
MBS	mortgage-backed security
MFA	Managed Funds Association
OTC	over the counter
PWG	President's Working Group on Financial Markets
SEC	U.S. Securities and Exchange Commission
SINBFC	systemically important nonbank financial company
SRO	self-regulatory organization

CHAPTER ONE

Introduction

In the wake of the financial crisis of 2007–2008, investors and policy-makers alike have called for renewed attention to hedge funds and their role in the financial system. In part, this interest has been prompted by recent insider-trading scandals at the Galleon Group hedge fund and other funds.[1] However, the interest also derives from deeper concerns about the role that hedge funds have come to play within the financial system and about a regulatory framework that may not effectively address the risk they pose to the financial system. The concern was articulated by the chairperson of the U.S. Securities and Exchange Commission (SEC) in 2009:

> [T]he road to investor confidence requires a concerted effort to fill the regulatory gaps that have become so apparent over the last 18 months. . . . One of the most significant gaps likely to be filled relates to hedge funds—which have flown under the regulatory radar for far too long. And without even a comprehensive database about hedge funds and their managers, it is virtually impossible to monitor their activities for systemic risk and investor protection purposes.[2]

---

[1] Raj Rajaratnam, head of the Galleon Group hedge fund, was arrested in October 2009 on charges of illegal insider trading. He was convicted of fraud, conspiracy, and violations of securities laws in May 2011. At one point, Galleon managed more than $7 billion in assets (Lattman and Ahmed, 2011).

[2] Schapiro, 2009.

Generally speaking, hedge funds cannot market their services to the general public and must either solicit funds only from large institutions and wealthy investors or limit ownership of their shares to 100 investors.[3] As a result, hedge funds have been exempt from many reporting and other regulatory oversight requirements while still being subject to restrictions against fraud.[4] As opposed to many other types of investment vehicles, such as mutual funds, hedge fund managers are free to pursue any investment strategy they choose.[5] The role hedge funds play in the financial system has attracted attention for multiple reasons. First, hedge funds have grown rapidly in the past 15 years. The number of hedge funds increased from roughly 3,000 to 9,500 between 1998 and 2010, and the assets under management (AUM) industry-wide grew from approximately $200 billion to $2.4 trillion.[6] Second, hedge funds invest in many of the complex financial instruments at the heart of the financial crisis of 2007–2008, including mortgage-backed securities (MBSs), collateralized debt obligations (CDOs), credit default swaps (CDSs), and short sales. Third, the high leverage and high trading volume characteristic of some hedge funds

---

[3]   High-net-worth individuals and institutions are presumed to be sophisticated investors who typically are either professional investors or receive professional investment advice. They are able to absorb more risk than the average investor, and, consequently, regulators have had a more hands-off approach to hedge funds.

[4]   For example, the advisers that manage hedge fund portfolios have, until recently, not been required to register with the SEC nor been subject to the consequent periodic SEC examinations. Even though the SEC does not have the authority to conduct periodic examinations of nonregistered advisers, it retains authority to conduct examinations for fraud at any investment adviser.

[5]   A mutual fund is a company that brings together money from many people and invests it in stocks, bonds, or other assets. Each investor in the fund owns shares, which represent a part of these holdings. Mutual funds must register with the SEC and are subject to investor-protection regulations, including regulations requiring a certain degree of liquidity, regulations requiring that mutual fund shares be redeemable at any time, regulations protecting against conflicts of interest, regulations to ensure fairness in the pricing of fund shares, disclosure regulations, and regulations limiting the use of leverage (SEC, 2008).

[6]   Data for 1998 are from U.S. Government Accountability Office (GAO), 2008, p. 1. Data for 2010 are presented in Chapter Two. *AUM* refers to the market value of hedge funds' capital, as distinct from the overall value of assets held by hedge funds, which can be much larger because of leverage.

are thought by some to exacerbate volatility of asset prices and instability of the financial system.[7] Finally, the lack of public information
about their operations and reduced regulatory oversight has meant that
hedge funds remain mysterious to many and are an easy target for
blame when there is a financial collapse.[8]

This report explores the extent to which hedge funds create or
contribute to systemic risk. By *systemic risk*, we mean the risk of a major
and rapid disruption in one or more of the core functions of the financial system caused by the initial failure of one or more financial firms
or a segment of the financial system.[9] The potential for a shock idio-
syncratic to a financial firm to be transformed into an aggregate shock
that affects the entire financial system is one useful way of thinking
about systemic risk.

To do this, we explore the role of hedge funds in the financial
crisis of 2007–2008. We also examine the response to and the consequences of the 1998 failure of Long-Term Capital Management
(LTCM), a large hedge fund. The failure of LTCM raised policymakers' and regulators' awareness of hedge funds as a potential source of
systemic risk. We also examine the extent to which the recent financial-
reform legislation, the Dodd-Frank Wall Street Reform and Consumer
Protection Act of 2010 and other recent regulatory changes, addresses

---

[7] See, for example, IMF, 2003, Chapter Three.

[8] See, for example, Brown, Green, and Hand, 2010, p. 2.

[9] This definition closely follows the definition used by the United Kingdom's Financial
Services Authority (FSA) (2011, p. 1). Olivier De Bandt and Philipp Hartmann arrive at a
similar definition, following their 2000 review of the systemic risk literature:

> A systemic crisis can be defined as a systemic event that affects a considerable number of
> financial institutions or markets in a strong sense, thereby severely impairing the general
> well-functioning of the financial system. . . . At the heart of the concept is the notion of
> "contagion", a particularly strong propagation of failures from one institution, market or
> system to another. (quoted in Billio et al., 2011, p. 1)

With regard to core functions of the financial system, the financial system channels house-
hold savings to the corporate sector and allocates investment funds among firms, it allows
intertemporal smoothing of consumption by households and expenditures by firms, and it
enables households and firms to share risks (Allen and Gale, 2001).

systemic risks posed by hedge funds.[10] Although of potential regulatory concern, the issues raised by hedge funds for investor protection are outside the scope of this analysis.[11] In addition, we do not examine in detail how the performance of hedge funds compares with that of other investment vehicles.

In the remainder of this introductory chapter, we review the pathways through which hedge funds may potentially contribute to systemic risk, the methods used in our analysis, and the organization of the report.

Potential Contribution of Hedge Funds to Systemic Risk

Hedge funds can contribute to systemic risk through two main channels: the credit channel and the market channel.[12]

Systemic risk arises through the credit channel when hedge fund losses result in default to creditors and the financial institutions with which they do business, and those losses go on to cause broader problems for the financial system. Hedge funds create exposures for financial institutions in several ways: They borrow, they make securities transactions, and they are often counterparties in derivatives trades.[13] If the losses at a single large fund or across multiple smaller funds are sufficiently large, then the losses could destabilize a creditor or counterparty,[14] which might be systemically important in its own right. For example, such an outcome could occur if a hedge fund's losses are so large that its capital is wiped out and a creditor has not required sufficient margin or collateral to protect itself against default.

Systemic risk through the market channel arises when hedge funds drive an unsustainable increase in asset prices during financial booms

---

[10] Public Law 111-203, signed into law July 21, 2010.

[11] Investor-protection issues include the accurate communication of investment strategies, rules for withdrawing investments, and equal treatment of similarly situated investors.

[12] FSA, 2010, p. 3.

[13] Stulz, 2007, p. 188.

[14] A counterparty is the other party that participates in a financial transaction.

or price drops that overshoot long-run market equilibrium in financial crises. Hedge funds can be significant investors in certain markets and are active traders in many markets. As a result, large funds, or common actions by a group of funds, may induce price increases that do not reflect market fundamentals. Conversely, forced selling by hedge funds may cause sharp price declines that ripple out to other financial firms in a vicious cycle.[15]

Research Methods

To conduct our research, we reviewed the literature on systemic risk and hedge fund contributions to systemic risk. We focused particular attention on analyses of the LTCM collapse and the financial crisis. Our investigation was informed by interviews with 45 people. The total breaks down as follows: 22 who worked in the hedge fund industry (including hedge fund investment advisers, lawyers representing hedge funds, staff of industry associations, and staff at firms that assemble and analyzed hedge fund data); eight congressional staffers; five financial regulators; five researchers and policy analysts; three prime brokers; and two institutional investors. Some people were interviewed multiple times. The interviews were conducted either in person or by phone using an open-ended interview protocol. The bulk of interviews were conducted during the first half of 2010, with some conducted after the passage of Dodd-Frank in July 2010. Interviews covered the ways in which hedge funds have contributed or can potentially contribute to systemic risk, strategies for reducing systemic risk, and, for those interviews conducted following the passage of Dodd-Frank, the implications of Dodd-Frank for the hedge fund industry. To encourage candor, the interviews were conducted on a confidential basis. Notes

---

[15] Stulz, 2007, uses *liquidity risk* and *volatility risk* to refer to the types of risks that are included here in the market channel. *Liquidity risk* refers to a situation in which too many funds have set up the same trades and may not be able to exit their positions quickly. In such a case, prices may overreact, and liquidity may fall sharply. *Volatility risk* refers to situations in which hedge fund investment strategies push prices away from fundamentals (Stulz, 2007, p. 188).

taken during the interviews were entered into a database that organized responses by topic areas, and the database was used to analyze interview responses.

Data on the hedge fund industry were purchased from eVestment|HFN.[16] eVestment|HFN collects self-reported information on more than 7,100 hedge funds, funds of funds, and commodity products.[17] For comparison, there were approximately 10,000 hedge funds worldwide in 2010 (see Chapter Two). eVestment|HFN provided information on such topics as the historical performance of hedge funds, the number of annual fund launches and liquidations, AUM, investor flows, the number of funds, and the distribution of funds by size.

Organization of This Report

Chapter Two provides background on hedge funds and the hedge fund industry. In addition to presenting trends in the size and structure of the industry, it describes the sources of investment funds and the types of investment strategies. Chapter Three describes the incident that first brought attention to the systemic risks associated with hedge funds: the failure of LTCM. The causes of the incident are described, as are the regulatory and industry responses. In Chapter Four, we investigate the role hedge funds played in the financial crisis of 2007–2008. Evidence of contributions through the credit channel is first examined, followed by evidence of contributions through the market channel. Chapter Five identifies concerns about how hedge funds might contribute to systemic risk moving forward. It also discusses whether and how Dodd-Frank and other recent reforms address the ways in which hedge funds can contribute to systemic risk. The chapter does not provide a detailed assessment of efficacy of the recent reforms because many are still in process but rather provides observations on whether key issues are being addressed and the gaps that remain. The report concludes (Chapter Six) with considerations that policymakers, regulators, and

---

[16] eVestment|HFN is part of eVestment Alliance.

[17] HedgeFund.net, undated.

analysts of the financial system should keep in mind as they consider and evaluate reforms that could affect the hedge fund industry. An appendix describes the regulatory reforms that address potential systemic risks.

CHAPTER TWO

Background on the Hedge Fund Industry

Hedge funds are a dynamic and innovative part of the U.S. and global financial systems.[1] They are one of several institutions involved in moving money from capital suppliers to capital users. This chapter provides an overview of the industry and outlines the features of hedge funds that tend to exacerbate and mitigate systemic risk.

Overview of the Hedge Fund Industry

Legal Structure and Role in the Financial System

Hedge funds in the United States are a type of private fund. A private fund is defined in terms of exemptions from certain federal securities laws and regulations that apply to other investment pools, such as mutual funds.[2] Dodd-Frank defines a private fund as "an issuer that would be an investment company, as defined in section 3 of the Investment Advisers Act of 1940 . . . , but for section 3(c)(1) or 3(c)(7) of the Act."[3] Section 3(c)(1) excludes funds that do not publicly offer their shares and whose shares are not owned by more than 100 investors. Section 3(c)(7) excludes funds whose shares are offered exclusively to "qualified" investors. Generally, qualified investors are individuals or

---

[1] Alfred W. Jones is generally credited with setting up the first hedge fund in 1949. See Mallaby (2010) for a description of the evolution of the hedge fund industry.

[2] GAO, 2008, p. 9.

[3] Pub. L. 111-203, §401.

companies that own at least $5 million and $25 million in investments, respectively.[4]

In a recent rulemaking, the SEC defines a hedge fund as any private fund that can

- pay its investment advisers a performance fee calculated by taking into account unrealized gains
- borrow in excess of one-half of its net asset value or may have gross investment exposure in excess of twice its net asset value
- sell securities or other assets short or enter into similar transactions (other than for the purpose of hedging currency exposure or managing duration).[5]

The first condition refers to the investment adviser's compensation plan, the second refers to the amount of leverage a fund can assume, and the third refers to the ability to sell short. We describe hedge fund practices in each of these regards in this section.

Most hedge funds are organized as limited partnerships established for the purpose of investing the money of their partners.[6] As is discussed in Chapter Six, Dodd-Frank has imposed restrictions on bank investments in hedge funds. A hedge fund will hire a professional investment adviser to manage its funds. The investment adviser is a separate legal entity and does not face the restrictions that hedge funds do in terms of the offering or ownership of shares. For example, an investment adviser can, in principle, be publicly traded and issue bonds.[7] Hedge fund advisers can be freestanding organizations or a part of a larger organization, such as a commercial or investment bank. Advisers are typically compensated using a "2 and 20" fee structure. Under this scheme, the annual management fee is set at 2 percent of AUM and typically is meant to cover operating costs. Managers also

---

[4]   GAO, 2008, p. 9.

[5]   SEC, undated (a), p. 11.

[6]   Edwards, 1999, p. 190.

[7]   One business unit of Citadel (a large hedge fund) serves as an investment adviser and has issued a five-year bond (Mallaby, 2010, p. 366).

receive 20 percent of profits as an incentive or performance fee. The compensation agreement often sets a "high water mark" or "hurdle rate" that must be met before the manager is able to receive an incentive fee.[8] The incentive fee is meant to more closely align the interests of the hedge fund manager with those of hedge fund investors and prevent the manager from taking undue risks with the fund's capital. Additionally, investors often require the hedge fund manager to personally invest in the fund.[9] However, it should be noted that, although advisers are rewarded for positive performance, they do not have to refund fees, nor are they penalized (say, by a fine), when profits are negative.[10]

As private funds, hedge funds are free to pursue any investment strategy they choose. They can invest in a wide range of financial assets, including equities, bonds, derivatives, futures contracts, commodities, currencies, and other assets. In contrast to mutual funds, hedge funds do not face restrictions on short selling, leverage, or concentrated positions. The term *hedge fund* initially came from investment strategies that built portfolios that were "market neutral" or "hedged." Managers following such strategies would take positions on the performance of one type of security relative to another in a way that immunized the portfolio from general market movements.[11] However, hedge funds

---

[8]   There is variability in the fees charged across the industry. Some hedge fund managers reduce fees for larger investments (Burton, 2010), and other hedge funds charge higher fees (e.g., 3 percent of net assets and 50 percent of profits). As a point of reference, the average fee paid to mutual fund managers is about 1.4 percent, and there is rarely any profit sharing. Broad-based index mutual funds tend to charge less than 0.25 percent and some less than 0.1 percent. Assets managed by a professional investment adviser are typically assessed a 1-percent management fee on AUM without any profit sharing (Stepleman, 2010).

[9]   SEC, 2003. Agarwal, Daniel, and Naik (2009, p. 2231) finds that the ratio of the manager's investment in a fund to the fund's AUM averages 7.1 percent. The figure is based on an analysis of 7,535 funds between January 1994 and December 2002 (funds were not necessarily in business throughout the entire period).

[10]   Of course, investment advisers will suffer in other dimensions when profits are negative. Investors can express their displeasure by withdrawing their assets (thus reducing the management fee), and, when profits are negative, the investment adviser will suffer losses on personal assets that are invested in the fund.

[11]   Edwards, 1999, p. 190.

today do not always hedge and can make large directional bets on the overall movement of the market.

Hedge funds are financial intermediaries in the sense that they participate in the markets that mediate the transfers of capital from suppliers to users. As such, they can contribute to, or detract from, the efficiency of financial markets. Hedge funds have significant connections to the largest actors in the financial system. Hedge funds use the prime brokerage and other services offered by large commercial banks and, until their conversion to commercial banks during the financial crisis, large investment banks.[12] The banks act as counterparties for a wide variety of hedge fund trades, extend hedge fund margin and other types of credit, execute trades, hold hedge fund collateral, and can be the repository for hedge fund assets.[13]

Number of Hedge Funds and Assets Under Management

Precise figures on the number of hedge funds are difficult to obtain, but, according to eVestment|HFN, a leading accumulator of data on the hedge fund industry, there were between 9,200 and 10,100 hedge funds worldwide as of 2010. As shown in Figure 2.1, the number of funds grew rapidly between 2003 and 2007 and then dipped appreciably during the financial crisis. After a slight increase in 2009, the upward trend resumed, and, by 2010, the number of hedge funds had roughly returned to the precrisis level. The number of funds in existence today is more than triple the estimated 3,000 in 1998.

AUM by the hedge fund industry worldwide more than doubled in the three years prior to the financial crisis, reaching just under $3 trillion in 2007 (Figure 2.2). This total is dramatically higher than the $200 billion estimated under management in 1998. Hedge funds were hit hard by the financial crisis. Between investor withdrawals

---

[12] A commercial bank is a bank whose main business is deposit-taking and making loans. In contrast, an investment bank's main businesses are (1) securities underwriting, (2) advising on mergers and acquisitions, (3) asset management, and (4) securities trading. A prime broker is an institution (or part of an institution) that offers various settlement, custody, and financing services to hedge funds and other specialized investment or dealing operations ("Financial Times Lexicon," 2012).

[13] Margin is borrowed money that is used to purchase securities.

Figure 2.1
Number of Hedge Funds

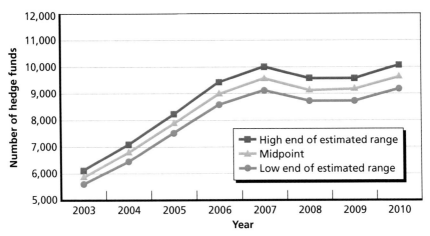

SOURCE: Data provided to the authors by eVestment|HFN.
NOTE: Excludes funds of funds (FOFs).
RAND MG1236-2.1

Figure 2.2
Assets Under Management by the Hedge Fund Industry

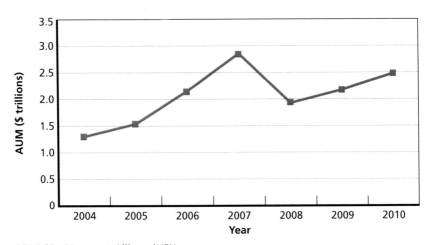

SOURCE: eVestment Alliance|HFN.
RAND MG1236-2.2

and losses on investments, AUM fell approximately 30 percent. Solid growth returned in 2009 and 2010.

In terms of AUM, hedge funds are small relative to other sectors of the financial system (see Figure 2.3). As of September 30, 2010, the global mutual fund industry managed $23.7 trillion in assets, and the top 50 U.S. bank holding companies alone had $14.4 trillion in assets.[14] By comparison, the global hedge fund industry had an estimated $2.5 trillion under management at the end of 2010.[15]

Even though hedge funds do not account for a large share of AUM economy-wide, they do account for a substantial volume of the trading activity in many markets. A 2007 study found that hedge

Figure 2.3
Assets Under Management by the Hedge Fund Industry Compared with Assets in Other Financial Sectors

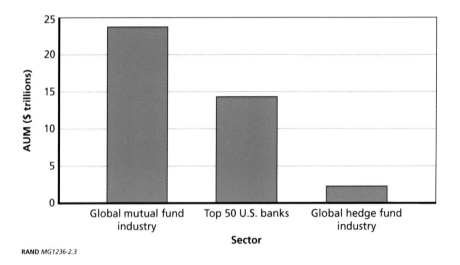

RAND MG1236-2.3

---

[14] Managed Funds Association (MFA), 2011, p. 3.

[15] Data from a periodic survey of hedge fund managers by the FSA suggest that the hedge fund positions do not account for a large percentage of asset value in most markets. The survey covers an estimated 20 percent of global hedge fund assets. In only three of the 12 asset markets examined did the sum of the long market value and the short market value controlled by the surveyed hedge fund managers exceed 1 percent of the gross notional value of the market (FSA, 2011, pp. 4–5).

funds accounted for 25 to 60 percent of the turnover in the markets examined (see Table 2.1). Frequent trades are integral to some hedge fund strategies, such as those that seek to take advantage of arbitrage opportunities.[16]

Restrictions on Investor Withdrawals from Hedge Funds

Hedge funds typically require investors to commit at least $1 million to the fund and usually put restrictions on when an investor can withdraw funds.[17] A common requirement is that investors agree not to withdraw new investments for one year (the initial lockup period) and then can only withdraw investments quarterly, after providing 60- to 90-day notice (the notice period). In addition, hedge funds often typically allow the investment manager to impose investment gates that limit the amount that an investor can withdraw from the fund at any one time or over a given period. According to knowledgeable parties in the industry with whom we spoke, gates that limit withdrawals to 25 percent of an investor stake in the fund or to 25 percent of the total

Table 2.1
Percentage of Market Turnover Accounted for by Hedge Funds

Asset	Percentage
Cash equities	30
Credit derivatives (plain)	60
Credit derivatives (structured)	33
Emerging market bonds	45
Distressed debt	47
Leveraged loan trading	33
High-yield bond trading	25

SOURCE: Blundell-Wignall, 2007, p. 42.

---

[16] Arbitrage is the practice of taking advantage of price differences between two or more similar assets or securities.

[17] Stulz, 2007, p. 179.

fund assets are common. Hedge funds can also set up "side pockets" for certain illiquid investments. Investors are not able to withdraw the capital that supports these investments until the investments mature or otherwise become marketable. Lockup periods, notice periods, gates, and side pockets allow hedge funds to invest using strategies that may take time to prove profitable. They also protect remaining investors from declines in asset prices caused by the rapid liquidation of positions that can be required to meet sudden withdrawal requests. These provisions can also protect hedge funds from cascading withdrawal runs: Without gates, investors that see other investors withdraw assets might attempt to withdraw assets before asset prices decline even further and the fund's assets are depleted, creating a self-reinforcing cycle.

Characteristics of Hedge Fund Investors

According to those with whom we spoke, institutional investors, such as pension funds and university endowments, have accounted for an increasing share of money flowing into hedge funds. According to their estimates, 75 to 80 percent of new money flowing into hedge funds in recent years has come from institutional investors. According to its survey of 60 hedge fund managers, Preqin estimates that 61 percent of AUM in 2011 was provided by institutional investors, up from 44 percent in 2008. Institutional investors include public pension plans (making up 16 percent of the funds from institutional investors), endowment plans (14 percent), private pension plans (14 percent), and foundations (11 percent).[18] Together, these four types of institutional investors account for 55 percent of institutional funds and roughly 33 percent of total AUM (0.55 times 0.61).[19] Individuals and families from a wide range of economic strata participate in or benefit from

---

[18] Preqin, undated. Institutional investors also include FOF (22 percent of the capital from institutional investors), family offices (5 percent), insurance companies (5 percent), and banks (3 percent). A family office is a private company that manages investments and trusts for a single wealthy family (Family Office Exchange, undated). Preqin provides information, products, and services to hedge funds, FOFs, investors, placement agents, and investment consultants.

[19] The total rises to 77 percent once FOFs are added. Pension plans, endowments, and foundations also invest in FOFs.

these plans, which belies the common perception that hedge funds benefit only wealthy individuals and families.

A fund of hedge funds (also known as an FOF) is a pooled fund that invests in multiple hedge funds (typically, 15 to 20 different hedge funds). This is attractive to some investors because FOF managers conduct due diligence on the individual hedge funds, and the multiple hedge funds present in the FOF provide diversification. If one hedge fund were to fail, the entire FOF would remain operational. Most FOFs are private funds and thus can provide services only to qualified investors or to a limited number of investors. The downside to investing in an FOF is the fees. In addition to paying the typical 2 and 20 to the individual hedge fund, the FOF also customarily takes a 1-percent management fee and a 10-percent performance fee. Thus, an investor could end up paying a 3-percent management fee and a 30-percent performance fee in order to invest in a portfolio of hedge funds.[20]

A sizable share of the assets managed by hedge funds flows through FOFs, but the percentage has dropped since the financial crisis began (see Figure 2.4). There are on the order of 3,000 FOFs industry-wide.[21]

Distribution of Funds in the Industry, by Size and Characteristics of Hedge Fund Advisers

Hedge funds vary enormously in size, and the largest funds account for a substantial fraction of the AUM industry-wide. As shown in Figure 2.5, approximately two-thirds of funds (amounting to 6,321 funds) have less than $100 million in AUM each, accounting for 7 percent of assets managed by the industry. In contrast, roughly 3.5 percent of funds (378 funds) manage $1 billion or more in assets each, and these funds account for 56 percent of the AUM industry-wide.[22]

---

[20] SEC, 2008a; Harper, 2009.

[21] Based on data from eVestment|HFN. The September 2011 FSA survey found a lower percentage of assets provided by FOFs: Overall, 28 percent of assets were provided by "other investment funds," which includes FOFs (FSA, 2011, p. 9).

[22] These figures are based on data from eVestment|HFN. eVestment|HFN suspects that the smallest funds are less well represented in its database than larger funds, so the percentage of funds with assets less than $100 million might exceed 66 percent. The percentage

Figure 2.4
Assets Managed by Funds of Funds as a Percentage of Assets Managed by Hedge Funds

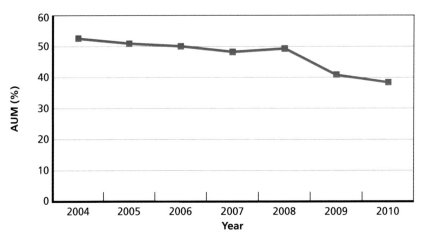

SOURCE: Data provided to the authors by eVestment|HFN.
RAND *MG1236-2.4*

Investment advisers can manage multiple funds. The largest hedge fund investment advisers in the industry as of June 2011 are listed in Table 2.2. Thirty-three advisers manage $10 billion or more in hedge fund assets.

Despite the fact that a small percentage of funds manage a substantial share of industry-wide assets, the hedge fund industry is not particularly concentrated. The largest hedge fund adviser manages assets equal to only approximately 3 percent of the entire hedge fund industry.[23]

---

of industry-wide assets managed by these funds might not be much greater than 7 percent, however, because the amount managed by each fund in this category is relatively small.

[23] MFA, 2011, p. 4. A common measure of industry concentration is the Herfindahl-Hirschman index (HHI). The HHI is the sum of the squared market shares for all firms in an industry, when a firm's market share is expressed in percentage points. If the market share of no firm in an industry exceeds 3 percent, the HHI cannot exceed approximately 300 (32 × 33.3). An industry whose HHI is less than 1,000 is considered "not concentrated" by the U.S. Department of Justice (DOJ) and Federal Trade Commission (FTC) (1997, p. 14).

Figure 2.5
Distribution of Funds and Assets Under Management, by Size of Fund

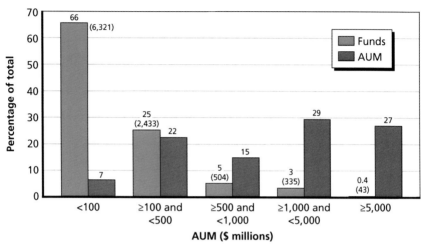

SOURCE: Data provided to the authors by eVestment|HFN.
NOTE: The numbers in parentheses indicate the number of funds. The figure covers
AUM as of April 2011
RAND MG1236-2.5

Table 2.2
Largest Hedge Fund Advisers, by Assets Under
Management Worldwide, as of June 30, 2011

Hedge Fund Adviser	AUM ($ billions)
Bridgewater Associates	59
Man Group	39
Paulson and Company	35
Brevan Howard	31
Och-Ziff Capital Management Group	29
BlueCrest Capital Management	27
JPMorgan Chase	26
Soros Fund Management	26
BlackRock	24

Table 2.2—Continued

Hedge Fund Adviser	AUM ($ billions)
Credit Suisse	24
Baupost Group	23
Winton Capital Management	21
Farallon Capital Management	20
Goldman Sachs	20
King Street Capital Management	20
Renaissance Technologies	20
Elliott Management	17
Appaloosa Management	16
AQR Capital Management	16
Canyon Partners	15
D. E. Shaw Group	15
Lansdowne Partners Limited	15
Moore Capital Management	15
York Capital Management	15
Citadel	14
Eton Park Capital Management	14
S. A. C. Capital Advisors	14
Viking Global Investors	14
Fortress Investment Group	12
Avenue Capital Group	11
Millennium Management	11
Tudor Investment Corporation	11
Anchorage Capital Group	10
Total	679

SOURCE: Pensions and Investments, 2011.

Hedge fund advisers are primarily based in the United States. According to Hedge Fund Intelligence, U.S.-based advisers manage 76 percent of global hedge fund assets, UK-based advisers manage 16 percent of global industry assets, and Hong Kong–based advisers manage 0.5 percent of global hedge fund assets.[24]

Hedge Fund Returns and Investment Strategies

Investors that invest in hedge funds typically find them attractive for two reasons: higher net returns and portfolio diversification. The institutional investors we interviewed explained that, as returns were decreasing from other investment strategies, they looked to investments in hedge funds as a way to increase overall returns. Hedge funds employ leverage, which can magnify gains in up markets but also compound losses in down markets. Hedge fund returns are often said to be uncorrelated with broad stock market indexes in part because of shorting strategies that allow funds to make money in down markets as well as in up markets.

Figure 2.6 shows the types of returns typically reported for the hedge fund industry as a whole.[25] As seen in the figure, hedge fund returns may not always exceed the returns of the broader equity market, but they have produced positive returns even when the broader market is down. Negative returns in 2008 dispelled the notion that hedge funds yield positive returns regardless of the performance of the overall market. Returns for the industry as a whole were off 16 percent in 2008, which, although a shock to many hedge fund investors, was not nearly as bad as the –37-percent return for the S&P 500®. And, according to the Dow Jones Credit Suisse Core Hedge Fund Index, hedge fund returns were –7.4 percent in 2011, nearly 10 percentage points

---

[24] As cited in SEC, 2012, pp. 11–12.

[25] The returns in Figure 2.6 consider funds that ultimately go out of business. However, lack of reporting by funds with low returns or that are about to go out of business will cause the reported figures to overstate the returns across the industry as a whole. Conversely, failure of very successful funds to report will cause the reported figures to understate industry-wide returns. How these two biases offset each other is difficult to assess.

Figure 2.6
Annual Returns for the Hedge Fund Industry and the S&P 500

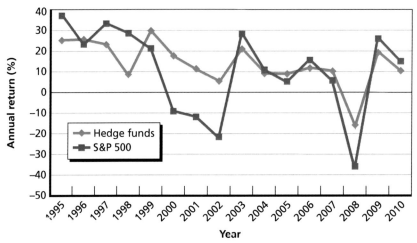

SOURCE: Hedge fund returns from data provided to the authors by eVestment|IIFN.
RAND *MG1236-2.6*

below the 2.1-percent total return for the S&P 500 in that year.[26] Of
course, the returns of individual hedge funds vary considerably, as do
returns on individual equities.

Evidence is not clear on how hedge fund performance compares
with returns on the main asset classes.[27] A recent study by KPMG
and the Alternative Investment Management Association (or AIMA,
a hedge fund industry association) found that the average hedge fund
delivered a 9.1-percent return per year between 1994 and 2011, compared with 7.2 percent for global stocks, 6.3 percent for global bonds,
and 7.3 percent for commodities. The return volatility was also lower
for hedge funds than for global stocks and commodities, although
higher than for bonds.[28] Ilia Dichev and Gwen Yu, in contrast, conclude that "the risk-return trade-off of hedge fund investors is much

---

[26] Credit Suisse Hedge Fund Index, undated; Standard and Poor's, 2012.

[27] We have not attempted a comprehensive assessment of hedge fund returns, and the magnitude of hedge fund returns is not of primary relevance to the issues addressed in this study.

[28] Centre for Hedge Fund Research, 2012, p. 9.

worse than previously thought."[29] Dichev and Yu examined returns for nearly 11,000 hedge funds from 1980 to 2008. They find that hedge fund returns are lower than the S&P 500 index and only marginally higher than the risk-free rate of return.[30]

Hedge funds invest in a broad array of assets. One-third of 2010 AUM was in funds that invest primarily in equities (see Table 2.3).

Table 2.3
Distribution of Assets Under Management, by Primary Asset
Class (%)

Primary Asset Class	2006 (total AUM = $2.154 trillion)		2010 (total AUM = $2.473 trillion)	
Equities	40		33	
Multiasset	34		38	
Fixed income	18		25	
Corporate		43		59
Mortgages		7		9
Government		8		6
Multitype or nonspecified		42		27
Commodities	3		3	
Other	5		2	
Total	100		100	

SOURCE: Data provided to the authors by eVestment|HFN.
NOTE: Because of rounding, columns may not total 100.

---

[29] Dichev and Yu, 2011, p. 249.

[30] Dichev and Yu, 2011. Dichev and Yu use dollar-weighted returns in their analysis rather than the more typical buy-and-hold returns used in the KPMG and AIMA analysis. Buy-and-hold returns measure the return of an investor that joined the fund at inception and has held the same position across time. The authors argue that such a measure does not accurately reflect returns of actual investors that join the fund sometime after inception and invest in uneven bursts of capital contributions. Dollar-weighted returns are weighted over time by the amount of invested capital, better reflecting, they argue, the timing and magnitude of fund flows on investor returns.

One-quarter of industry assets are in funds that primarily invest in fixed-income assets, with the majority of those in corporate securities. A small percentage of AUM is in funds that invest primarily in commodities. A substantial portion of assets is in funds that indicate that they do not invest primarily in one asset class (i.e., multiasset funds). It should be noted that even funds that primarily invest in one asset class might still hold assets in other classes.

Hedge funds provide investors access to short investments, but by no means do hedge funds shun long investments. Table 2.4 breaks down AUM by the directional bias indicated in the self-reported descriptions of a hedge fund's investment approach. A much higher percentage of the AUM industry-wide is in funds that have invested long only or have a long bias than in funds that have a short bias. However, a substantial share of assets is in funds that can invest short or long (the *variable bias* or *relative value* categories), as well as in funds that do not provide enough information to determine the directional bias of their portfolio (the *not specified* category). Short investments are an important component of hedge fund investment strategies, but it is

Table 2.4
Distribution of Assets Under Management, by Directional Bias of Portfolio (%)

Directional Bias	2006 (total AUM = $2.154 trillion)	2010 (total AUM = $2.483 trillion)
Long only	6	7
Long bias	19	13
Variable bias	11	9
Short bias	0.4	0.2
Relative value	33	38
Not specified	31	32
Total	100	100

SOURCE: Data provided to the authors by eVestment|HFN.
NOTE: Because of rounding, columns do not sum to 100.

not possible with the data in Table 2.4 to determine the share of assets in short positions versus long positions.

Hedge funds pursue a wide range of investment strategies. As shown in Table 2.5, the largest percentage of AUM is in funds whose primary strategy is long and short equity investments. A long-short equity hedge fund takes both long and short positions on stocks, attempting to identify undervalued and overvalued stocks. Such funds often attempt to hedge their positions against market risk so that the fund is protected against movements in the market as a whole. Event-driven strategies and funds that focus on emerging markets are the next most prevalent. Event-driven funds attempt to take advantage of opportunities created by mergers and acquisitions and other business transactions.[31] Hedge funds will also make investments in areas shunned by other investors, thereby providing a useful service in "completing" financial markets. As shown in Table 2.5, for example, some hedge funds specialize in distressed assets, helping to stabilize the prices of assets that might otherwise continue to fall. More-regulated investment pools, such as mutual funds, have strict limits on leveraging, portfolio diversification requirements, and liquidity requirements that allow them to pay redemptions at any time. These requirements restrict their ability to move nimbly in the marketplace and pursue a wide range of arbitrage opportunities.

Hedge funds use leverage in their investment strategies. Roughly speaking, *leverage* refers to the market value of all positions held by the fund (both long and short) divided by equity capital.[32] Leverage allows hedge funds to earn a significant return on investor capital even when the profit on an individual transaction is small. Hedge fund leverage is difficult to calculate because of the lack of publicly available information and the difficulty of determining what exactly should be included in the leverage calculation. For example, substantial leverage can be

---

[31] Stulz, 2007, p. 182. Global macro funds are based on an analysis of macroeconomic variables and invest in all types of assets and markets. Convertible arbitrage exploits the mispricing of convertible debt instruments. Fixed-income arbitrage exploits mispricing in bond and other interest rate instruments (Strömqvist, 2009, pp. 88, 98).

[32] See Ang, Gorovyy, and van Inwegen (2010) for definitions of *hedge fund leverage*.

Table 2.5
Distribution of Assets Under Management, by Primary Investment
Strategy (%)

Primary Investment Strategy[a]	2006 (total AUM = $2.154 trillion)	2010 (total AUM = $2.473 trillion)
Long-short equity	30	22
Event driven, special situations	12	21
Emerging markets[b]	10	12
Multiple strategy	11	11
Distressed assets	6	8
Commodity trading advisers[c]	6	8
Global macro	6	8
Fixed income, arbitrage	5	5
Fixed income, directional	3	2
Convertible arbitrage	3	2
Market-neutral equity	3	2
Statistical arbitrage	1	2
Options strategies	0.4	0.3
Total[d]	97	103

SOURCE: Data provided to the authors by eVestment|HFN.

[a] A fund's primary investment strategy is based on descriptions provided by the fund.

[b] Funds can be in this category as well as a second category.

[c] Also known as managed futures.

[d] Columns do not sum to 100 because not all strategies are listed and funds can be in both the emerging markets category and a second category. Also, because of rounding, the totals are not exact.

embedded in derivatives, but practices differ on how to include this intrinsic leverage in an overall leverage measure.

A recent study suggests that hedge fund leverage is modest for the industry as a whole. Ang, Gorovyy, and van Inwegen find that the leverage ratio averaged 2.1 for the industry as whole between December 2004 and October 2009, with a high of 2.6. By comparison, the leverage ratio of investment banks over the same period was 14.2, with a high of 40.7 in 2009.[33] In its 2009 and 2010 surveys, the FSA found that the leverage of the hedge fund managers surveyed ranged between roughly 2.5 and 3.0.[34]

Leverage, of course, varies across funds. Hedge Fund Research reported in 2011 that approximately one-third of all funds do not use leverage and that more than half of all funds utilize leverage between one and two times their investment capital. The hedge fund analysis firm also found that larger funds typically employ higher leverage, with 23 percent of funds with more than $1 billion in AUM carrying leverage ratios of between 2.0 and 5.0.[35] Leverage can be higher in certain industry segments. For example, funds that focus on fixed-income arbitrage were leveraged between 6.0 and 14.0 in the 2009 and 2010 FSA surveys, and, as we will see in the next chapter, the leverage for LTCM rose to levels much higher than that.[36] Such outliers could be driving the perceptions that the typical hedge fund is highly leveraged.

Hedge funds can borrow money in several ways, including borrowing from prime brokers, repurchase agreements (*repos*), and the synthetic borrowing embedded in financial instruments, such as total return swaps.[37] The hedge funds participating in the 2010 FSA survey (recall that the participating funds are primarily UK-based) relied

---

[33] Ang, Gorovyy, and van Inwegen, 2010. The authors warn, however, that their analysis is based on data self-reported by hedge funds and that the hedge funds in their sample of firms use different definitions of *leverage*.

[34] FSA, 2011, p. 7.

[35] Hedge Fund Research, 2011.

[36] FSA, 2011, p. 7.

[37] In a repo, the borrower sells a financial security to the lender with the promise to buy it back at a fixed price on a specified date. The security itself serves as collateral for the loan. The difference between forward price and the spot prices is the interest rate on the loan. A total return swap allows a hedge fund to obtain the total return on the asset (interest plus capital gains) without buying the asset. The hedge fund will pay the seller a fixed interest rate for the total return swap plus any negative changes in asset value. The hedge fund will typically post some collateral that is less than the value of the asset, thereby generating leverage (Commodities Futures Trading Commission [CFTC] and SEC, 2011, p. 97).

heavily on repos, with roughly 53 percent of borrowing coming from this source. Collateralized borrowing from prime brokers accounted for only 17 percent of the total, and synthetic borrowing accounted for 30 percent.[38]

Attributes of Hedge Funds That Amplify and Mitigate Their Potential Contribution to Systemic Risk

Several characteristics of hedge funds amplify their potential contribution to systemic risk. First, although leverage for the industry as a whole appears modest, the leverage of some funds can be high. High leverage by hedge funds can contribute to systemic instability. Second, hedge fund investments can be very risky, allowing for large losses that cascade through the financial system. Third, hedge funds can invest in highly specialized financial instruments for which there are relatively few buyers and sellers. Liquidity in such thin markets can rapidly disappear, causing steep declines in asset prices when a hedge fund decides to or is forced to sell. Finally, information on hedge fund positions is not readily available. Contributing to the problem are SEC rules that, until recently, have discouraged hedge funds from providing public information about their strategies and operations.[39] The lack of information makes it difficult for creditors, counterparties, and regulators to assess, much less address, the risks posed by hedge funds.

---

[38] FSA, 2011, p. 6.

[39] Hedge funds have not been able to market their securities via any general solicitation or general advertising. The SEC defines *general advertising* as "any advertisement, article, notice, or other communication published in any newspaper, magazine, or similar media or broadcast over television or radio; and any seminar or meeting whose attendees have been invited by any general solicitation or general advertising" (SEC Rule 502[c], promulgated under the Securities Act of 1933). According to several industry experts we interviewed, the result has been that hedge funds have been reluctant to post information on their web sites and to respond to questions from the press. Of course, even without such a rule, hedge funds may be reluctant to publicly reveal much information about their investment strategies, returns, or operations. As is discussed in Chapter Six, Congress recently instructed the SEC to revise this rule.

Several hedge fund characteristics serve to mitigate their potential contribution to systemic risk. First, as discussed earlier, hedge fund assets are modest compared with those in other sectors of the financial system, such as banks and mutual funds. Second, lockup periods, notice periods, gates, and side pockets can limit pressures on hedge funds to liquidate their positions in down markets.[40] These restrictions protect funds from the equivalent of a run on the bank. Finally, some hedge fund characteristics can provide incentives for careful risk management:

- The hedge fund manager typically invests in the fund.
- Hedge fund managers have no access to the Federal Reserve's discount window and thus have no lender of last resort.
- Institutional investors and FOFs are the source of a sizable share of hedge fund assets. These institutional investors and FOFs have the resources to carefully monitor the risk-management practices of the hedge funds in which they invest. They therefore can provide a form of private-sector oversight of the hedge fund industry.

---

[40] As is discussed in Chapter Four, an industry participant with whom we spoke estimated that on the order of 30 percent of hedge funds raised gates during the financial crisis.

CHAPTER THREE

The Collapse of Long-Term Capital Management

Between January and September 1998, LTCM lost nearly all of its value. Financial-system regulators concluded that the rapid failure of one of the then-largest U.S. hedge funds might destabilize world financial markets and coordinated a private-sector buyout of the firm. LTCM's failure raised awareness among regulators, banks, and other actors in the financial system that hedge funds could be a source of systemic financial risk. This chapter examines the factors that caused the collapse of LTCM and the policy response.

Factors Leading to the Collapse of Long-Term Capital Management

During the second half of the 1990s, LTCM pursued a strategy of "fixed-income arbitrage," which exploited short-term differences in government bond prices that were expected to eventually converge.[1] For example, the fund bet that the prices of government bonds that were issued at different times but with the same maturity would converge. This convergence trade extended to exploiting temporary price differentials between stocks listed on multiple exchanges (for example, Royal Dutch versus Shell).

The LTCM strategy worked well in a calm world, but the financial world was anything but calm in the second half of the 1990s. A

---

[1] Stulz, 2007.

financial crisis hit east Asia in 1997, and Russia threatened to default on its sovereign debt in 1998. Investors fled to safe assets, and the spreads on government bond prices widened rather than narrowed. LTCM suffered losses as a result, and the losses were compounded by its high leverage. Its ratio of assets over equity was more than 25, a very high number that was much higher than the leverage for the industry as a whole.[2] LTCM was also a very large player in many of the markets in which it took positions. This made it difficult to liquidate positions when it needed to raise capital to cover losses, further contributing to its collapse. Between January and September 1998, the fund lost $4.6 billion, or 90 percent of the $5 billion it had in capital.

LTCM was able to achieve such a high level of leverage in large part because of practices in the derivatives market and in the market for repurchase agreements. With regard to the derivatives market, its counterparties did not require it to post margin on many of its over-the-counter (OTC) derivatives trades.[3] These OTC trades were often not cleared through central clearing facilities. Inadequate "haircuts" (percentage of market value subtracted from assets used as collateral) on repurchase agreements also allowed it to build leverage. As with many hedge funds, LTCM did the bulk of its borrowing in the repo market. LTCM would sell an asset to an investment bank or other counterparty with the promise to buy it back later. A haircut reduces the risk to the seller that the underlying asset declines in value during the course of the repurchase agreement.[4] Inadequate haircuts provided LTCM with more borrowed funds and, at the same time, did not protect the lending parties from LTCM default.

---

[2] Edwards, 1999.

[3] President's Working Group on Financial Markets (PWG), 1999.

[4] For example, a 2-percent haircut would mean that the borrower would receive only $9.8 million on collateral valued at $10 million at the time of the trade (Barbican Consulting, undated).

The Rescue of Long-Term Capital Management

Federal regulators were concerned that an LTCM failure posed systemic risk through both the credit and market channels. Regarding the credit channel, they feared that default by LTCM could threaten the solvency of several major banks and securities firms. As far as the market channel is concerned, regulators feared that default could trigger a fire-sale liquidation of positions held by large financial institutions that were similar to LTCM's.[5] They were concerned that the drop in prices would then force other leveraged investors to sell off assets as the value of their collateral fell below the amounts they had borrowed.[6] The fear was that LTCM's collapse would spread to investors with no relationship to LTCM.[7] Regulators were also concerned that credit and derivatives markets could cease to function "for a period of one or more days and maybe longer."[8] Some financial institutions were already fragile at that time. According to one observer, there were rumors that Lehman Brothers was on the verge of bankruptcy, and regulators were worried that an LTCM failure would push Lehman over the edge.[9]

To limit potential damage due to a chaotic unwinding of the fund, the Federal Reserve of New York facilitated an infusion of $3.6 billion to LTCM by a group of private banks (which included nearly all of the top commercial and investment banks). These banks took over LTCM's positions, and LTCM investors lost their investment.

---

[5]   Financial Crisis Inquiry Commission (FCIC), 2010, p. 20.

[6]   Edwards (1999, pp. 199–200) reports,

> News that LTCM and possibly other hedge funds were in trouble . . . set off alarm bells throughout the financial community. These funds, under pressure to meet margin calls and to provide more collateral to creditors and swap counterparties, might be forced to sell their large holdings at any price, which would collapse the value of these securities.

[7]   FCIC, 2011, p. 57.

[8]   McDonough, 1998, as quoted in FCIC, 2011, p. 57.

[9]   Mallaby, 2010, p. 241.

The Aftermath of the Collapse of Long-Term Capital Management

The LTCM episode demonstrates that there are risks associated with a high degree of leverage and that hedge funds can be systemically important.[10] The LTCM episode prompted assessments of what went wrong and recommendations regarding what should be done to avoid similar situations in the future. The recommendations, by and large, did not favor direct regulation of hedge funds. Rather, they focused on greater market discipline of hedge fund operations and indirect regulation through already-regulated entities, such as banks that provided prime brokerage services for hedge funds.[11]

In its report on LTCM and systemic risk, GAO blamed inadequate risk management by banks and securities firms for the development of a situation that posed systemic risk to the financial system:

> LTCM was able to establish leveraged trading positions of a size that posed potential systemic risk primarily because the banks and securities and futures firms that were its creditors and counterparties failed to enforce their own risk management standards.[12]

The PWG concluded that the LTCM episode "illustrates the need for all participants in our financial system, not only hedge funds, to face

---

[10] One should not conclude based on the LTCM experience that the failure of any large hedge fund can threaten the financial system. The failure of Amaranth Advisors provides an example. Amaranth specialized in natural gas futures and, at its peak, had $9 billion in AUM, nearly double the $5 billion LTCM had under management at the beginning of 1998. It collapsed in September 2006 after losing nearly $5 billion in natural gas trading. The Amaranth collapse, however, does not appear to have had widespread impacts on the financial system or broader economy (see discussion in Mallaby, 2010, pp. 310–322; and Shadab, 2009, p. 3).

[11] *Indirect regulation* refers to a situation in which federal regulators regulate the banks and other institutions that provide credit to hedge funds and serve as hedge fund counterparties and these parties, in turn, oversee hedge funds.

[12] GAO, 1999, p. 29.

constraints on the amount of leverage they assume."[13] Like GAO, they noted that investors, creditors, and counterparties did not provide an effective check on LTCM's overall activities. They did praise financial institutions for tightening credit risk management subsequent to LTCM's collapse but feared that practices would relax as the LTCM episode receded from memory. To reduce the possibility of similar events in the future, the PWG recommended, among other things, that

- more-frequent and meaningful information on hedge funds be made public
- financial institutions enhance their practices for counterparty risk management
- regulators encourage improvements in the risk-management systems of regulated entities.

The PWG further concluded that, if these indirect means of controlling hedge funds and other then-unregulated market participants were not effective in constraining excessive leverage, "several other matters" should be given further consideration—an oblique reference to more-direct control of hedge fund leverage.[14]

Later in 2006, Federal Reserve chairman Ben Bernanke underscored the perception that oversight of hedge funds by banks and broker-dealers had improved:

> Since the LTCM crisis, ongoing improvement in counterparty risk management and the resultant strengthening of market discipline appear to have limited hedge fund leverage and improved the ability of banks and broker-dealers to monitor risk, despite the rapidly increasing size, diversity, and complexity of the hedge fund industry. Many hedge funds have been liquidated, and

---

[13] PWG, 1999, p. 29. Established by executive order in 1988, the PWG is charged with enhancing the integrity, efficiency, orderliness, and competitiveness of U.S. financial markets and with maintaining investor confidence.

[14] PWG, 1999, p. viii.

investors have suffered losses, but creditors and counterparties have, for the most part, not taken losses.[15]

Those with whom we spoke during the course of this study believe that prime brokers and other hedge fund creditors have done a good job controlling the potential credit risks of hedge funds in the aftermath of the LTCM crisis. The risk of hedge fund losses to prime brokers and other creditors is perceived to be low because of the imposition of adequate margin and collateral requirements and oversight of hedge fund leverage.

According to those we interviewed, there was some concern among financial regulators that standards were beginning to weaken during the boom years preceding the financial crisis. Cause of such possible weakening could include competition among prime brokers for hedge fund business during the boom years and new entrants into the prime-brokerage business that had not gone through the LTCM experience. In response, the Federal Reserve conducted a horizontal review of hedge fund prime brokers in 2005–2006. The review reinforced the importance of maintaining acceptable collateral and clearing derivatives and other transactions in a timely fashion. As is made clear in the next chapter, this type of indirect regulation did appear to be adequate during the financial crisis as far as credit risk is concerned: There is little evidence that hedge fund losses resulted in substantial losses for their creditors.

Although the PWG's recommendation for enhanced prime-broker oversight was implemented, little progress was made on the PWG's recommendation for more-frequent and meaningful information on hedge funds. It was not until after the financial crisis that Congress directed regulators to collect more information from hedge funds.

---

[15] Bernanke, 2006.

Lessons from the Collapse of Long-Term Capital Management

Several lessons can be drawn from the LTCM collapse. First, the collapse demonstrates the dangers of high leverage and very large positions. *High leverage* means that losses can quickly decimate capital. Very large positions make it difficult to liquidate positions without downward pressure on prices. Even though LTCM did not have to liquidate these positions, the fear of what would happen if it did so drove regulators to act.

Second, the LTCM experience also demonstrates that the indirect oversight of hedge funds by prime brokers and other counterparties can break down. Prime brokers were either unwilling or unable to restrain LTCM leverage and the accumulation of huge positions in particular markets. Focus on near-term profits can make prime brokers unwilling, and operations outside the purview of prime brokers can make them unable.[16] Even though the LTCM collapse demonstrates that indirect oversight of hedge funds can be ineffective, the track record in the ensuing years also illustrates that indirect oversight can work, at least as far as the credit channel for systemic risk is concerned. As indicated by Bernanke's statement quoted in the previous section, there appear to have been few cases post-LTCM in which hedge fund losses have cascaded into losses to creditors.

Third, the LTCM experience illustrates the importance of imposing appropriate margin requirements on derivatives. Had the derivatives in the 1990s been centrally cleared by an organization that enforced appropriate margin requirements, the LTCM debacle may never have occurred.

Finally, the experience of LTCM demonstrates the difficulty of fully understanding the risks posed by hedge funds. Information on

---

[16] As the PWG observed in 1999, even if prime brokers fully understood the risk of their investments, their motivation is to protect themselves but not the system as a whole (1999, p. 31). Other theories could also explain a lack of attention to the effects that their actions could have on systemic risk. For example, as the previous crisis recedes into the past, prime brokers with imperfect memory may think it less and less likely that the financial system will collapse any time soon.

hedge fund positions was not available to regulators or the public. It was only partially available to the prime brokers with which they do business: Hedge funds often use multiple prime brokers, and no one prime broker might see a hedge fund's entire book. Hedge funds can borrow in multiple markets and make very diverse and complicated investments. Complicating the problem is the fact that hedge funds can adjust positions very rapidly, making the positions difficult to follow. The secretiveness of hedge funds regarding their strategies and positions made it difficult for regulators and their creditors to fully understand the credit and market risks they posed.

CHAPTER FOUR

Hedge Funds and the Financial Crisis of 2007–2008

The financial crisis of 2007–2008 was the worst financial meltdown in the United States since the Great Depression. The crisis precipitated a major decline in output and unemployment from which the economy is still recovering as of this writing. Hedge funds were active participants in many of the financial markets and instruments closely linked to the financial crisis, and it is appropriate to ask whether they contributed to the collapse. This chapter examines whether and how hedge funds may have helped precipitate the financial crisis. This chapter begins with a brief overview of the factors underlying the crisis, followed by an analysis of the extent to which hedge funds contributed to the crisis through the two channels of systemic risk identified in Chapter One: the credit and market channels.

Factors Underlying the Financial Crisis

Before examining the role of hedge funds in the financial crisis, it is useful to step back and review the fundamental drivers of the crisis.[1] A root cause of the financial crisis lies in the imbalances in the world's economies that led to massive capital flows into the United States from China, Japan, and other countries. These inflows, combined with the Federal Reserve's loose monetary policy, resulted in very low interest rates. These low interest rates fueled growth in borrowing and set

---

[1] See FCIC (2011) for a detailed examination of the causes of the financial crisis.

the stage for the growth of a housing bubble. Also enabling the crisis was the growth of private-label securitization of residential mortgages. Under this "originate-to-distribute" model, lenders would originate mortgages and then sell them to investment banks and others that would package them into MBSs.[2] These securities were then sold to investors. Even though banks used this mechanism to transfer loans off their balance sheets, they still retained some exposure to the mortgages: They held mortgages that were still in the securitization pipeline and held on to some parts, or tranches, of MBSs that they could not sell. The originate-to-distribute model spread risk broadly and tapped a broad range of investors, but it also created incentives to weaken lending standards. Because the mortgage originators no longer kept the bulk of mortgages on their books, they had less incentive to maintain strict lending standards.

The markets for MBSs and the CDOs that were constructed from them would not have thrived without favorable ratings from the major credit-rating agencies.[3] Credit-rating agencies gave AAA ratings to many of the tranches of these securities under assumptions that turned out to be inaccurate.[4] Further contributing to the conditions that enabled the financial crisis were the financing strategies used by some large banks and other investors. High leverage and the reliance on short-term debt meant that relatively small changes in asset prices could quickly spiral into major price drops. Finally, investors often relied on CDSs to protect against the possibility of default on MBSs or CDOs.[5] These CDSs were issued by the insurance firm American International Group (AIG) and others, and the availability of this type of insurance

---

[2] FCIC, 2011, p. 89.

[3] CDOs are bundles of asset-backed securities. The asset-backed securities can be based on mortgages, bonds, or other types of loans. CDOs are sliced into layers, or tranches, based on the credit risk of the underlying assets.

[4] FCIC, 2011, pp. xxv, 426. Credit ratings by Standard and Poor's, for example, range from AAA to D, with bonds or other securities rated below BBB– considered junk bonds or speculative investments.

[5] CDSs require the seller to compensate the buyer in the case of default on a specified loan or debt instrument.

lent a sense of security that allowed the CDO and MBS markets to continue their growth. It turned out, however, that AIG had posted inadequate capital to back this insurance.[6] When the number of mortgage defaults began to increase and the credit-rating agencies finally began to downgrade the MBSs and CDOs, AIG quickly collapsed. In the final analysis, the financial instrument that had, in part, allowed the housing bubble to inflate offered little in the way of protection.

Against this backdrop, we investigate the extent to which hedge funds contributed to the financial crisis.

Hedge Fund Contribution to the Financial Crisis Through the Credit Channel

As discussed in Chapter One, hedge funds can contribute to a major breakdown of the financial system through the credit channel. Such an outcome can occur when hedge fund losses destabilize creditors that are systemically important. In this section, we explore the extent to which hedge funds contributed to the financial crisis through the credit channel.

Impact of Hedge Fund Losses on Creditors

Hedge funds suffered substantial losses during the financial crisis. Returns on AUM were –16 percent in 2008, shocking many who thought that hedge funds were structured to produce returns even in a down market (see Figure 2.6 in Chapter Two).[7] For example, Citadel, a Chicago-based hedge fund, had $13 billion under management in 2007. By the end of 2008, its two flagship funds were down by $9 billion, the equivalent of nearly two LTCM failures.[8] In addition, a substantial number of hedge funds were liquidated during the financial crisis. As shown in Figure 4.1, approximately 1,700 hedge funds

---

[6] FCIC, 2011, p. 50.

[7] Recall from Chapter Two that the S&P 500 fell 37 percent in 2008.

[8] Mallaby, 2010, pp. 308, 370.

Figure 4.1
Number of Hedge Fund Launches and Liquidations

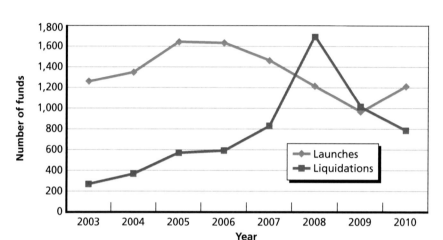

SOURCE: Data provided to the authors by eVestment|HFN.
RAND *MG1236-4.1*

were liquidated in 2008, or about 18 percent of the approximately 9,500 funds in the preceding year.[9]

There is little indication, however, that hedge fund losses during the financial crisis led to significant losses at prime brokers and other creditors. Informed parties with whom we spoke did not believe that hedge fund losses resulted in major losses to their creditors, and such knock-on (ripple or follow-on) effects are not highlighted in the analyses of the financial crisis that we have reviewed. It appears that the prime brokers and other creditors, for the most part, required adequate margin and collateral to protect themselves against hedge fund losses. In this sense, the prime brokers appear to have learned from the failure

---

[9] Liquidations include hedge funds that go out of business and return assets to investors (accounting for 65 percent of liquidations in the eVestment|HFN database between 2003 and 2010), funds that have notified eVestment|HFN that they will no longer report data because of poor performance (8 percent), funds that merged with other funds or are restructured (3 percent), and funds that eVestment|HFN is unable to contact (21 percent). It would be useful to obtain data on what fraction of industry assets the liquidated funds managed at their peak.

of LTCM.[10] The efforts by prime brokers, reinforced by bank regulators, to more carefully monitor the credit risk of hedge funds and to more rigorously enforce collateral and clearing requirements appear to have paid off.

In spite of their losses, hedge funds were not the recipients of taxpayer bailout money, at least directly. In this sense, the hedge funds that did go out of business were not viewed as too big to fail by government regulators.

The Failure of the Bear Stearns Hedge Funds

Even though hedge funds do not appear to have contributed significantly to the financial crisis through the credit channel, the collapse of two Bear Stearns hedge funds in the spring of 2007 resulted in substantial losses for Bear Stearns, an organization that was viewed as systemically important and did subsequently fail. Bear Stearns was not a major creditor of the Bear Stearns hedge funds, so the hedge funds did not create a major credit risk for Bear Stearns. However, Bear Stearns did bail out the hedge funds out of concern that the failure of these entities could raise investors' concerns about the firm itself.[11] In that sense, the hedge funds created a type of reputational risk for Bear Stearns.

By the mid-2000s, Bear Stearns had become the leading securitizer of MBSs on Wall Street. As part of its efforts to expand its mortgage packaging business, Bear Stearns bought subsidiaries that made subprime mortgages directly to home buyers and set up two internal hedge funds that loaded up on MBSs and CDOs.[12] The Bear Stearns funds were leveraged 10 or 15 to 1 and targeted assets that were rated AA or AAA. The hedge funds financed the purchase of these assets by borrowing on the repo market, which, as discussed previously, was not uncommon for hedge funds.[13] Repo lenders in May 2007 sent low

---

[10] It is also worth noting that the lessons from LTCM may not have been lost on hedge fund managers.

[11] FCIC, 2011, p. 240.

[12] Mallaby, 2010, pp. 335–336.

[13] FCIC, 2011, p. 135.

marks on the value of the CDOs and MBSs in the portfolios of the Bear Stearns hedge funds. These low marks triggered margin calls, and the funds had to sell assets at distressed prices to raise cash. This led to a loss of confidence by fund investors, increasing redemption requests and creating the need to sell additional assets. Bear Stearns ultimately decided to rescue the hedge funds, probably to protect the Bear Stearns brand. In the end, Bear Stearns essentially bought out the repo lenders for approximately $1.6 billion. By July 2007, the Bear Stearns hedge funds had lost all their value.[14]

The failure of the Bear Stearns hedge funds did appear to have some broader impacts on the larger financial system. The failures caused significant losses for Bear Stearns, an investment bank that would need to be rescued by JPMorgan Chase and U.S. taxpayers less than a year later.[15] The failure of the Bear Stearns hedge funds also raised concerns among financial market regulators. During a June 2007 meeting of the Federal Reserve Bank's Federal Open Market Committee (FOMC), Chairman Bernanke noted that the situation faced by the Bear Stearns hedge funds was a good example of how high leverage can decrease the liquidity of a hedge fund's portfolio, especially when creditors and counterparties fail to provide the fund with adequate time to liquidate positions. Some FOMC members were concerned about the lack of transparency regarding hedge fund positions and the consequent lack of discipline in the valuation of hedge fund holdings. Others were concerned about the lack of information about Bear Stearns' counterparties. Finally, there were concerns that the Federal Reserve could not systematically collect information from hedge funds because they were outside the Fed's jurisdiction.[16]

The collapse of the Bear Stearns hedge funds also highlights problems that can arise when hedge funds are run within larger institutions. The parent organization can feel the need to bail out failing funds,

---

[14] FCIC, 2011, pp. 239–241.

[15] The Federal Reserve lent JPMorgan Chase $29 billion as a condition of its takeover of Bear Stearns (Mallaby, 2010, p. 336). JPMorgan Chase repaid the loan with interest in June 2012 ("AIG Repays Bailout from N.Y. Fed," 2012, p. B2).

[16] FCIC, 2011, p. 241.

exacerbating any weakness in the parent. If the parent institution has many linkages within the financial system, there may be consequences for systemic risk. If it is considered too big to fail and bailed out by the government, there may be consequences for taxpayers.

Hedge Fund Contribution to the Financial Crisis Through the Market Channel

Although there is little evidence that hedge funds contributed to the financial crisis through the credit channel, the story is much more nuanced regarding their contribution to the financial crisis through the market channel. In this section, we explore the extent to which hedge funds contributed to the crisis or mitigated systemic risk through the market channel during the financial crisis. We first examine the role hedge funds played in the markets for MBSs and CDOs, two markets that were at the heart of the financial crisis. We then turn to evidence on whether hedge fund deleveraging contributed to the downturn in asset prices, followed by an examination of hedge fund involvement in the short selling to which analysts often point as a driver of the crisis. Finally, we examine the extent to which withdrawal of hedge fund assets from investment banks contributed to the collapse of these institutions.

Hedge Fund Contribution to the Buildup of the Housing Bubble

MBSs and CDOs played a role in providing capital for the subprime-mortgage market. Attracted by returns that ranged from 15 to 30 percent, hedge funds often purchased the equity tranches of MBSs and CDOs. However, data on the role hedge funds played in the MBS and CDO markets are fragmentary, and different analyses come to different conclusions on the importance of hedge funds in this market.

Figures presented by International Monetary Fund (IMF) director John Lipsky in July 2007 indicated that hedge funds held only 10 percent of the equity tranches in the CDO market, and Houman Shadab of the Mercatus Center estimates that hedge funds accounted for, at most, 8 percent of the CDO market in 2007.[17] In contrast, analysis by the FCIC suggests that hedge funds played a significant role in the CDO market during the run-up to the financial crisis. The FCIC estimates that more than half of the equity tranches of CDOs issued in the second half of 2006 were purchased by hedge funds.[18] The investments in the equity tranches of the MBSs and CDOs made the creation of the more–highly rated tranches possible and thus arguably contributed to the real estate bubble.[19] But it should be recognized that other sectors of the financial industry also invested in the equity tranches of these derivatives. Lipsky reports that higher percentages were held by banks (31 percent), insurers (19 percent), and pension funds (18 percent).[20]

The equity tranches of CDOs were known to be risky, and losses on these tranches were not at the heart of the financial crisis. What drove the financial crisis were losses on the investment-grade tranches. Hedge funds also invested in these tranches. The FCIC report tells of hedge funds that bought the tranches of CDOs rated AAA or AA and used them as collateral in repo agreements but does not provide estimates of the magnitude of hedge fund investments in the investment-

---

[17] Shadab (2008, p. 9) estimates that hedge funds accounted for $70 billion of the $900 billion CDO market. eVestment|HFN tracks AUM of funds whose primary focus is on securitized mortgage assets. The amount of AUM ranged from $20 billion to $30 billion from 2004 through the first half of 2009 ("Strategy Focus Report," 2011). However, it is difficult to translate these figures into the hedge fund share of the MBS and CDO markets. Note first that leverage will mean that the positions held will be greater than the AUM. Also, funds whose primary focus is not on securitized assets might also invest in mortgage-related assets, and, conversely, funds that invest primarily in mortgage-related assets might invest in other types of assets as well.

[18] An FCIC survey of more than 170 hedge funds that together managed more than $1.1 trillion in assets as of early 2010 found that, by June 2007, the largest hedge funds held $25 billion in the equity and other lower-rated tranches of MBSs (FCIC, 2011, p. 192).

[19] It is worth noting that a relatively small amount of hedge fund capital can enable a large amount of CDOs to be issued. The equity tranches accounted for perhaps 20 percent of a typical CDO. The hedge funds that invested in CDOs were thought to be leveraged anywhere from six to ten in 2005–2007 (Shadab, 2008, p. 9). Combining these two figures implies that $1 million in hedge fund capital could support up to $50 million of CDOs.

[20] Lipsky, 2007.

grade tranches.[21] Lipsky estimates that hedge fund investments were roughly evenly split between the equity and nonequity tranches of CDOs but notes that the hedge fund share of the overall CDO market was small.[22]

Although some hedge funds were long in MBSs and CDOs, managers who bought equity tranches often hedged their investments by shorting the more-senior tranches. The FCIC survey found that $25 billion in equity and other lower-rated tranches purchased by hedge funds was offset by $45 billion in short positions. Several hedge funds made large bets against the subprime-mortgage sector in 2005, 2006, and 2007.[23] Hedge funds also played an important role in uncovering the exposure of financial institutions to subprime mortgages.[24]

There was a great deal of activity and turmoil during the financial crisis in the sector of the hedge fund industry that invests in MBSs. eVestment|HFN reports an "[o]verwhelming failure of funds that focused on leveraged exposure to securitized assets."[25] During our interviews, we heard that many hedge funds whose primary strategies did not involve buying CDOs or MBSs were lured into the market by the large returns. Many such funds made money for a while but ultimately suffered significant losses. Some of those funds failed as a result, and the stronger funds absorbed the losses and returned to their primary strategies. At the same time that a substantial number of hedge funds in the MBS sector were failing, a spike in launches of hedge funds that invest in this sector occurred. eVestment|HFN reports that launches of funds that focus on MBSs or securitized credit peaked in 2008, which coincided with the lowest number of launches for the overall hedge fund industry in eight years.[26] eVestment|HFN noted that many of

---

[21] FCIC, 2011, pp. 117, 135.

[22] The nonequity tranches taken as a whole are much larger than the equity tranches, so the Lipsky figures imply that the hedge fund share of the nonequity tranches is considerably below 10 percent.

[23] Mallaby, 2010, pp. 323–331; Lewis, 2010.

[24] FCIC, 2011, p. 234.

[25] "Strategy Focus Report," 2011.

[26] "Strategy Focus Report," 2011.

these funds were launched to take advantage of the dislocations in the securitized markets during the crisis. Because hedge funds are opportunistic by nature and, as mentioned earlier, help to "complete" financial markets, this phenomenon is not surprising. It is likely that this repopulation of funds contributed to the relatively attractive returns for this sector in 2008. As shown in Figure 4.2, hedge fund returns on mortgage-related assets were down in 2008 but remained positive.

Figure 4.3 shows the net inflow of investor funds into hedge funds between 2004 and 2010 whose primary asset class was mortgage-related bonds. As can be seen, there was an outflow during 2007, when the housing bubble was beginning to deflate, but a substantial inflow during the first half of 2008, when the housing market was in free fall.[27] There was also an increase in investor inflows in 2009. How hedge funds invested these inflows is unknown, but the figures at least

Figure 4.2
Returns on Funds That Focus on Mortgage-Backed Securities

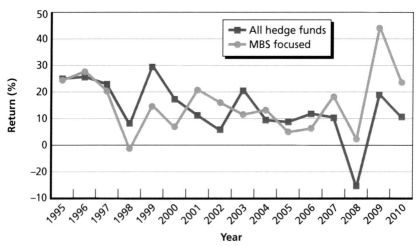

SOURCE: Data provided to the authors by eVestment|HFN.
RAND MG1236-4.2

---

[27] Total AUM in this category was $25 billion to $30 billion in 2007 and 2008, so a $3 billion flow is about 10 percent of AUM. Note that these figures are before leverage is applied, so the total exposure of hedge funds in these markets would be much higher.

Figure 4.3
Net Investor Inflows into Funds Whose Primary Asset Focus Is Fixed-Income Mortgages

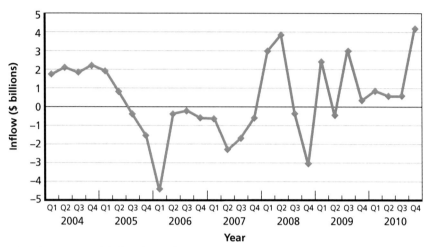

SOURCE: Data provided to the authors by eVestment|HFN.
RAND *MG1236-4.3*

suggest that hedge funds remained active participants in these markets and might have helped limit the decline in asset prices during the financial crisis.

The MBS and CDO markets were at the heart of the buildup of the mortgage bubble, and hedge funds were active long investors in these markets. Thus, one might argue that hedge funds contributed to market volatility by helping inflate the housing bubble. However, hedge funds invested on both sides of the subprime-mortgage market and played an important role in calling attention to the housing bubble. Some hedge funds invested in assets that were based on inaccurate ratings from credit-rating agencies and careless residential mortgage lending practices. Conversely, by shorting MBSs and bank stocks that were heavily exposed to the subprime market, hedge funds called attention to the cracks in the system and perhaps helped deflate the housing bubble before it grew larger. They also provided funds to this market at the trough of the crash, possibly limiting further declines. In light of these opposing factors, no strong case can be made that hedge funds were a significant contributor to the financial crisis through the buildup of the housing bubble. Other factors, such as the behavior of the credit-rating agencies, the availability of inadequately backed CDSs, and careless lending practices appear to be far more important.

Hedge Fund Deleveraging

In reaction to substantial losses in MBSs, Wall Street banks began to reduce the credit available to some highly leveraged hedge funds in the summer of 2008. At the same time, hedge funds faced unprecedented withdrawals by their investors. These forces created pressures on hedge funds to sell assets during the peak of the financial crisis, potentially contributing to the rapid decline in asset prices. Rapid declines in asset prices can create self-reinforcing cycles of margin calls, additional asset liquidations, and further price declines.

According to the FCIC survey, investor redemption requests (requests by investors to withdraw their investments from the hedge fund) averaged 20 percent of client funds in the fourth quarter of 2008.[28] Data from eVestment|HFN show that investor withdrawals industry-wide from the third quarter of 2008 through the first quarter of 2009 amounted to 4, 16, and 11 percent of AUM in the previous quarter, respectively (see Figure 4.4). The withdrawal of capital and credit required hedge funds to sell a large amount of assets, contributing to the glut of debt securities on the market and declines in asset prices.[29] Ben-David, Franzoni, and Moussawi find that hedge funds reduced their *equity* holdings by about 15 percent, on average, in each of the last two quarters of 2008. These reductions translate into 0.4 percent of total market capitalization in each of the last two quarters of 2008. In contrast, they find that sales of stocks by mutual funds during the crisis, as well as investor withdrawals, were an order of magnitude smaller than those of hedge funds.[30]

Declines in asset prices induced margin calls, which created further pressure to sell assets. The FCIC report tells of hedge funds

---

[28] FCIC, 2011, p. 361.

[29] FCIC, 2011, p. 361; Pozen, 2010, p. 119.

[30] Ben-David, Franzoni, and Moussawi, 2012, pp. 3, 46.

Figure 4.4
Investor Flows by Primary Asset Class (flow as percentage of AUM in previous quarter)

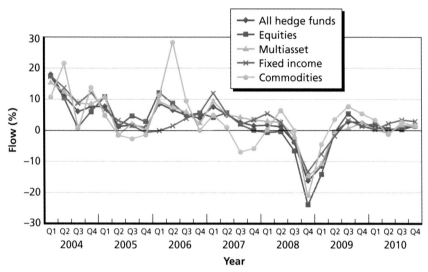

SOURCE: Data provided to the authors by eVestment|HFN.

RAND *MG1236-4.4*

that bought the tranches of CDOs that were rated AAA or AA and used them as collateral in repo agreements. When increased mortgage defaults led rating agencies to downgrade the tranches, hedge funds were faced with margin calls. These hedge funds were forced to sell, contributing to the glut of securities.[31]

Several analysts have concluded that hedge funds contributed to the decline in equity prices during the financial crisis. For example, Brown, Green, and Hand conclude that

> some, but certainly not most hedge funds may have been forced to liquidate portfolios into a falling market which could have worsened the financial crisis. While the timing of the abnormally low performance [i.e., hedge fund returns] does not appear to implicate hedge funds in the initial stages of the crisis, some evidence is

[31] FCIC, 2011, pp. 135, 213.

consistent with hedge fund portfolio activity increasing the duration and severity of subsequent decline in the overall market.[32]

Ben-David, Franzoni, and Moussawi conclude that hedge fund
selling in equity markets "may have amplified the initial negative
shocks to asset prices, and it certainly did not stabilize markets." They
also conclude that "hedge funds rushed to sell the most liquid securities
in their portfolios, suggesting that they tried to limit the price impact
during fire sales." They conclude that a large part of hedge fund selloffs
can be explained by investor redemptions and hedge funds responding
to lenders' pressure to deleverage.[33]

Recounting this sequence of events is not meant to imply that the
asset sales by hedge funds were unjustified. The initial buildup of hedge
fund positions in the nonequity tranches of CDOs was supported by
what turned out to be inaccurate credit ratings. Once the ratings were
corrected as subprime mortgages began to go bad, it was appropriate
for hedge funds to sell assets, both to exit from positions for which the
return was not commensurate with the risk and to meet margin calls.

Leverage plays a central role in determining how much downward
pressure there is on prices due to an initial adverse event.[34] As discussed
in Chapter Two, hedge fund leverage overall appears to be modest.
Even though some hedge funds are highly leveraged, hedge fund leverage does not stand out as a central contributor to the financial crisis.
Ang, Gorovyy, and van Inwegen find that hedge fund leverage started
to decrease prior to the first signs of the financial crisis in mid-2007,
even as the leverage of investment banks and the financial sector as

[32] Brown, Green, and Hand, 2010, p. 18.

[33] Ben-David, Franzoni, and Moussawi, 2012, pp. 6, 46–47.

[34] Suppose that a hedge fund has a leverage target of five and that it starts with $100 million
in assets and $20 million in investor capital. If an asset price falls by $5 million, its capital
would decrease to $15 million. To maintain leverage at five, the asset holdings would have to
fall to $75 million, resulting in a need to sell $25 million in assets. The higher the leverage,
the more severe the sales requirement would be.

a whole continued to increase. At the peak of the crisis in late 2008, investment banks had the highest leverage.[35]

Liquidity also plays an important role in determining how much downward pressure there is on prices due to an initial adverse event. *Liquidity* generally refers to the ability to trade large quantities quickly, at low cost, and without moving the price.[36] An asset can be illiquid because of uncertainty in its value, with MBSs and CDOs during the financial crisis providing good examples. It can also be illiquid when investors hold a large number of similar positions and want to exit the positions simultaneously or in large quantities relative to the typical level of transactions. Such "crowded trades" can result from herd behavior or concentration of hedge fund positions in a particular sector.

When assets are illiquid, a financial shock, such as an increase in the default rate on mortgages, can induce a liquidity spiral. In a liquidity spiral, margin calls generate the need to sell assets, and the lack of liquidity means that prices fall when assets are sold and price volatility increases, leading to further margin calls.[37] Hedge funds may be able to reduce their exposure to a liquidity spiral if their investments are diversified across multiple sectors and thus can avoid selling assets in the distressed markets. They may also reduce their exposure if they have longer-term financing that allows them to avoid selling at distressed prices or can impose gates to limit investor withdrawals.

Prices may have declined in equity markets because of changes in underlying fundamentals, but the markets appeared to remain liquid. In contrast, according to those with whom we spoke, other hedge fund investments that appeared to be liquid precrisis turned out not to be so

---

[35] Ang, Gorovyy, and van Inwegen (2010, p. 23) find that the highest level of gross hedge fund leverage was 2.6 in June 2007. In contrast, the leverage of investment banks was 10.4 in June 27, spiking upward to reach a peak of 40.7 in February 2009.

[36] Pástor and Stambaugh, 2003, p. 644. An illiquid asset is an asset that is not readily salable because of uncertainty about its value or the lack of a market in which it is regularly traded. An illiquid asset can also be thought of as an asset that cannot be sold at its underlying value (which, of course, may be subject to much disagreement).

[37] See Brunnermeier and Pedersen (2008) for the sequence of events that can lead to a liquidity spiral.

during the crisis. In particular, MBSs and CDOs became quite illiquid during the financial crisis.

It is difficult to determine the extent to which hedge funds were forced to sell in illiquid markets, further deepening the financial crisis. Lockup periods, notice periods, withdrawal gates, and side pockets served to shield hedge funds from illiquid markets during the financial crisis. Data on the number of funds that imposed gates or on the magnitude of investor withdrawals deferred are not readily available, but parties with whom we spoke indicated that on the order of 30 percent of funds imposed gates. In spite of lockup periods, notice periods, gates, and side pockets, investor withdrawals from hedge funds during the height of the financial crisis were substantial, although perhaps lower than they would have been without these withdrawal barriers.

Using a finding that hedge funds did not use all their sales proceeds to meet investor redemption requests, Boyson, Helwege, and Jindra conclude that there is scant evidence that hedge funds were forced into fire sales during the financial crisis.[38] However, Ben-David, Franzoni, and Moussawi respond that hedge funds may have needed to sell in order to reduce leverage, as well as to fund investor withdrawals.[39] In a previous paper, Ben-David, Franzoni, and Moussawi also conclude that hedge funds were not significant providers of liquidity during the financial crisis and, like other important actors in financial markets, provide liquidity in a procyclical fashion.[40]

Some hedge funds were clearly exposed to a liquidity crunch. For example, the Bear Stearns hedge funds had short-term financing that required them to sell assets in illiquid markets. However, better data are needed to understand the prevalence of this phenomenon during the financial crisis.[41]

---

[38] Boyson, Helwege, and Jindra, 2011, p. 2.

[39] Ben-David, Franzoni, and Moussawi, 2012, p. 6.

[40] Ben-David, Franzoni, and Moussawi, 2010, p. 32.

[41] The recent FSA surveys report information on the percentage of hedge fund portfolios that can be liquidated in a specified number of days in relation to the investor or financing liabilities that fall due over the same period (FSA, 2011, p. 8). We are not aware of similar data for hedge funds in the United States during the financial crisis.

It is difficult to come to strong conclusions about the extent to which hedge fund deleveraging contributed to the financial crisis. There is evidence that hedge funds contributed to downward price pressure and withdrew liquidity in some markets, but it is hard to assess how substantial these effects were. What is more, the investor inflows into funds that invest primarily in mortgage-related securities (see Figure 4.3) provide evidence that hedge funds also *injected* liquidity into some markets.

Short Selling

Short selling is a central part of many hedge fund investment strategies, and hedge fund shorting has been blamed for contributing to the financial crisis.[42] Richard S. Fuld Jr., chairman of Lehman Brothers, accused hedge funds of shorting Lehman stock and then distorting the firm's financial situation. The SEC's ban on shorting financial stocks between September 19 and October 8, 2008, indicates that at least some in government were concerned about the impact of short selling.[43]

Shorting can serve productive purposes. It allows an investor to offset risks in its portfolio. It allows investors to directly take a negative position on a stock rather than indirectly expressing such a view by declining to buy the stock. It dampens "irrational exuberance" and provides incentives for short sellers to investigate the true health of a firm, rather than rely on sometimes-misleading firm pronouncements. Finally, short selling can provide useful signals to the market when the

---

[42] In a conventional short sale, the short seller first borrows the stock from a third party for a lending fee, promising to return an equal number of shares at an agreed-upon time. The short seller then sells the stock at the prevailing market price. It later buys an equivalent number of shares prior to return to the lender. If the stock price declines a sufficient amount between the sale and subsequent purchase, the short seller makes money. A short seller essentially sells first and then buys. Long investors do the reverse.

[43] Christopher Cox, SEC chairman during the financial crisis, said that the biggest mistake of his tenure was agreeing to the three-week ban on short selling. Cox said that he was under intense pressure from then–Treasury Secretary Henry Paulson and Federal Reserve Chairman Bernanke to take this action and did so reluctantly (Paley and Hilzenrath, 2008).

firm itself is not forthcoming with information or provides incomplete information.

On the negative side, shorting, when public information about the true financial conditions of an asset or firm is incomplete, can create the appearance that a securities price is falling due to failing firm performance when, in fact, the firm remains healthy. And short sellers have a financial incentive to emphasize problems with the assets they are shorting in public and private communications. Goldstein and Guembel develop a model in which shorting can drive down the real value of the firm, enabling the short seller to profit on its position.[44] The possibility thus arises that short selling can force economically productive companies out of business. Although no single short seller might be large enough to materially affect a firm's stock price, there is the potential for a bear raid by a group of hedge funds that brings down a healthy company.[45] Such herd behavior is not necessarily the result of collusion among hedge funds; rather, it can result from multiple hedge funds acting on the same information in a similar manner.

Prior to the financial crisis, short selling had been constrained by the uptick rule. The uptick rule was initially adopted by the SEC in 1938. The rule required that a short sale be made either at a price above the security's last traded price or at the last traded price, if that price is higher than the price of the previous trade. The SEC eliminated the uptick rule in July 2007, citing results from a pilot study that the uptick rule was not necessary to prevent stock-price manipulation but reduced liquidity. Except for the ban on shorting approximately 1,000 mainly

---

[44] Goldstein and Guembel develop a scenario in which firm managers infer that short sales reflect negative information about a particular investment opportunity and therefore decide not to invest. They refer to such a trading strategy as "manipulation" (2008, p. 134).

[45] According to the SEC, a

"bear raid" involves the active selling of a security short to drive down the security's price in the hope of convincing less-informed investors of a negative material perception of a security, triggering sell orders. Falling prices could trigger margin calls and possibly force liquidations of the security, depressing the price further. This unrestricted short selling could exacerbate a declining market in a security by eliminating bids, and causing a further reduction in the price of a security by creating an appearance that the security's price is falling for fundamental reasons. (SEC, 2007, p. 11)

financial stocks for three weeks in September and October 2008, there were no restrictions on short selling during the financial crisis.

Pozen analyzes the role short selling played in the decline and failure of financial institutions during the financial crisis. He notes that chief executive officers (CEOs) often blamed unwarranted short selling for falling stock prices and concludes that, in some cases, short selling played an important role in forcing down the stock prices of these companies but, in other cases, did not. Pozen, for example, finds that a bear raid was a substantial contributor to the rapid decline in Lehman's stock price in September 2008. However, he finds little support for Merrill Lynch's contention that short selling caused a downward spiral in the firm's stock price during the same period. Pozen concludes that short selling can contribute to financial turmoil, but whether it does so in any particular instance is an empirical question.[46]

Misra, Lagi, and Bar-Yam present evidence of what they refer to as *manipulative short selling* in the fall of 2007. They see evidence of a bear raid in the very large jump in the number of borrowed Citigroup shares on November 1, 2007, followed by large decline in the number of borrowed shares on November 7, 2007. The authors conclude that manipulative short selling may have played a key role in the financial crisis.[47] Uncertainty remains, however, about the role hedge funds played in these short sales: The data used by Misra, Lagi, and Bar-Yam do not allow them to determine the extent to which the short selling was done by hedge funds as opposed to other financial actors.[48]

---

[46] Pozen, 2010, pp. 106–108.

[47] Misra, Lagi, and Bar-Yam, 2011, p. 2.

[48] Naked short selling exacerbated the downsides of short selling during the financial crisis, according to some with whom we spoke. In a naked short sale, the short seller agrees to sell a stock without owning it. The short seller must then go out and purchase or borrow the stock within the clearing period. If the short seller does not deliver the share to the buyer, the short seller is considered to have "failed to deliver" (SEC, 2008c). Naked short sales can put extra downward pressure on a stock because, in principle, the practice allows an unlimited number of shares to be sold short. Naked short selling is illegal, but it is difficult to determine how well the ban is enforced. (Statistics are available on failures to deliver, but naked short sales are not the only reason for a failure to deliver.) Some industry observers with whom we spoke believed that there was a massive failure to deliver on short sales during the financial crisis. However, we have not been able to determine the extent to which this was the case, whether

Although some studies identify short selling as a significant contributor to the financial crisis, the bulk of research does not conclude that short selling played a major role. Research and consulting firm Oliver Wyman reports that "it has since been shown by major broker-dealers that hedge funds were most likely net long position holders" of the affected financial firms in the fall of 2008 and that "the downward pressure [on their stocks] was a result of the selling off of long positions by traditional managers."[49] According to an analysis of hedge fund returns, Brown, Green, and Hand do not find "support for the hypothesis that opportunistic short-selling by hedge funds drove down prices and either created or magnified systemic risk in financial markets."[50] Although their analysis does not rule out the possibility that a small number of funds conducted intensive opportunistic short selling, they conclude that rampant and opportunistic bear raids did not occur.[51]

Studies of the effects of the short selling ban also do not indicate short selling as a major cause of the crisis. According to a detailed analysis of stock price data, Harris, Namvar, and Phillips found that the ban caused substantial price increases in financial stocks that had experienced negative price pressure prior to the ban. They also found that the price increases reversed approximately two weeks following the termination of the ban. However, the authors do not conclude that the short-selling ban allowed prices to more accurately reflect fundamentals but rather that the ban created a bias toward long sellers, with the unintended consequence of a substantial transfer from buyers to sellers.[52] Other studies find that the ban had little effect on prices. Boehmer, Jones, and Zhang conclude that the short-selling ban did little to boost returns of the firms on the ban list, and Oliver Wyman concludes that "the short selling bans [in the United States and the UK] had at best a

---

failure to deliver was more common during the crisis than prior to the crisis, or the extent to which hedge funds contributed to the problem.

[49] Oliver Wyman, 2010, p. 7.

[50] Brown, Green, and Hand, 2010, p. 11.

[51] Brown, Green, and Hand, 2010, p. 4.

[52] Harris, Namvar, and Phillips, 2009, p. 30.

neutral effect on prices."[53] These conclusions imply that the extremely troubled fundamentals of the major financial firms, rather than short selling, explain the declines in their stock prices. Boehmer, Jones, and Zhang emphasize the benefits of short selling, finding that "stocks subject to the ban suffered a severe degradation in market quality, as measured by [bid-ask] spreads, price impacts, and intraday volatility."[54]

Overall, there is limited evidence that shorting by hedge funds was a major contributor to the financial crisis. The banks' financial problems were much more directly related to their exposure to toxic mortgage assets and investor realization of the extent of this exposure than to the short selling of their stocks by hedge funds.

Hedge Fund Runs on Investment Banks

During 2008, hedge funds withdrew tens of billions of dollars in assets from investment banks. These withdrawals were essentially a run on the bank, analogous to bank runs by individual depositors during the Great Depression.[55] Experts with whom we spoke cited hedge fund runs on the investment banks as a causative factor of the financial crisis.

In early 2008, hedge funds that used Bear Stearns prime brokerage services were concerned that Bear would not be able to return their cash and securities. As a result, hedge funds withdrew assets and assigned trades they had done with Bear to other counterparties. The assets held by Bear's prime brokerage business fell from $160 billion in January 2008 to $90 billion in April 2008.[56] In the fall of 2008, hedge

---

[53] Boehmer, Jones, and Zhang, 2009, pp. 16–17; Oliver Wyman, 2010, p. 7.

[54] Boehmer, Jones, and Zhang, 2009, pp. 16–17. In contrast to Harris, Namvar, and Phillips, Boehmer, Jones, and Zhang find that the short-sale ban did little to boost returns of the firms on the ban list. The bid-ask spread is basically the difference between the highest price that a buyer is willing to pay for an asset and the lowest price at which the seller is willing to sell it.

[55] Diamond and Dybvig develop a model of the banking sector that shows that, in the absence of deposit insurance, banks are vulnerable to runs. They conclude that much of the economic damage in the Great Depression was caused directly by bank runs (Diamond and Dybvig, 1983, p. 404). Federal deposit insurance was made available through the Federal Deposit Insurance Corporation (FDIC) in the midst of the Great Depression to prevent such runs.

[56] FCIC, 2011, pp. 286–287.

funds withdrew tens of billions of dollars in assets from the remaining investment banks (Goldman Sachs, Lehman Brothers, Morgan Stanley, and Merrill Lynch), unsure of these banks' exposure to toxic mortgage assets. According to the FCIC, they moved the assets to commercial banks with prime brokerage services because they perceived that the commercial banks had a more diverse source of liquidity than investment banks, including access to the Fed's discount window. They also viewed the commercial banks as more transparent.[57]

Even though hedge fund withdrawals arguably contributed to the weaknesses of some investment banks, there were valid reasons for the actions. Hedge funds were concerned that their assets could be frozen if the investment bank that held them declared bankruptcy. Some hedge fund assets were not segregated from the investment bank's other assets, and prime brokers were able to use their clients' assets as collateral for their own activities.[58] As a consequence, assets could be tied up in bankruptcy proceedings.[59] Such a worst-case scenario did indeed occur in Lehman's September 2008 bankruptcy. As a result of the bankruptcy, at least $65 billion of assets held by the firm's London-based prime brokerage business were frozen.[60] In the two weeks that followed the Lehman bankruptcy, hedge funds pulled $128.1 billion from Morgan Stanley's prime brokerage business. By the end of September, the Federal Reserve had lent $107 billion to Morgan Stanley, at least in part because of the hedge fund withdrawals.[61] Reversing the

---

[57] FCIC, 2011, pp. 355, 360. Ivry, Keoun, and Kuntz (2011) documents the enormous borrowing from the Federal Reserve during the financial crisis.

[58] There are rules regarding the segregation of customer assets for securities (under SEC Rule 15c3-3) and for futures (under the regulations for Futures Commission Merchants) in U.S. banks. However, prior to Dodd-Frank, there were no rules for derivatives, which were generally excluded from the definitions for securities or futures, and banks in foreign jurisdictions typically face little in the way of segregation requirements. A good deal of Lehman's operations were in London. According to a hedge fund industry expert with whom we spoke, London customers were offered segregated accounts but declined them in return for more-favorable brokerage terms.

[59] FCIC, 2011, p. 360.

[60] Keoun, 2011.

[61] Keoun, 2011.

standard chain of events that could threaten financial-system stability, hedge funds now needed to be concerned about the counterparty risks posed by their prime brokers rather than prime brokers being concerned about the credit risks posed by hedge funds.

Assessment of Hedge Fund Contributions to the Financial Crisis

Our analysis does not identify hedge funds as primary contributors to the financial crisis. The roles played by mortgage lenders, credit-rating agencies, and inadequately backed CDSs were far more important. A broad range of analysts have come to similar conclusions. Strömqvist argues that hedge funds had more trouble handling the financial crisis than previous crises and concludes that hedge funds were more affected by the crisis than the crisis was affected by hedge funds. She does not rule out the possibility, however, that hedge funds, *together with banks and other institutional investors*, played a role in the development of the crisis.[62] Litan observes that hedge funds may have contributed to the demand for CDOs but that some funds profited enormously by betting against securities backed by subprime mortgages. He then concludes that hedge funds cannot be blamed for the crisis.[63] Mallaby argues that the real culprits of the financial crisis were off-balance-sheet structured investment vehicles owned by banks, leveraged broker-dealers, and a leveraged insurer (AIG), not hedge funds.[64] The FCIC does not emphasize the role played by hedge funds in its analysis of the crisis. Shadab observes that the closest hedge funds came to being a root cause of the financial crisis was the CDO market but concludes that hedge funds were never the primary driver in this market.[65] Finally, according to an analysis of the monthly returns of hedge fund indexes and portfolios of publicly traded banks, insurers, and brokers, Billio et al. argue

---

[62] Strömqvist, 2009, pp. 97, 104.

[63] Litan, 2010, p. 223.

[64] Mallaby, 2010, p. 245.

[65] Shadab, 2008, p. 8.

that the banking and insurance sectors may be more-important sources of systemic risk than hedge funds and brokers. They conclude that "the illiquidity of bank and insurance assets, coupled with the fact that banks and insurers are not designed to withstand rapid and large losses (unlike hedge funds), make these sectors a natural repository of systemic risk."[66]

---

[66] Billio et al., 2011, p. 38.

CHAPTER FIVE

Potential Hedge Fund Threats to Financial Stability and Reforms to Address Them

Although hedge funds did not play a pivotal role in the financial crisis, our examination of the crisis reveals ways in which they can potentially contribute to systemic risk. Similarly, our review of the LTCM episode illuminates potential threats to financial-system stability. From this analysis, we identify six areas of concern regarding hedge funds' potential contribution to systemic risk moving forward:

- lack of information on hedge funds
- lack of appropriate margin in derivatives trades
- runs on prime brokers
- short selling
- compromised risk-management incentives
- lack of portfolio liquidity and excessive leverage.

We then examine the extent to which these concerns are addressed by Dodd-Frank and other recent regulations.

Potential Hedge Fund Threats to Financial Stability

Lack of Information on Hedge Funds

Concerns about the lack of information on hedge funds were raised during the financial crisis. Regulators complained about the lack of transparency in hedge fund positions, leverage, and asset valuation and were frustrated by their inability to collect data on hedge funds. The secretiveness of hedge funds regarding their strategies and positions made it difficult for regulators and their creditors to fully understand the credit and market risks they pose. Following the LTCM collapse, the PWG recommended that more-frequent and meaningful information on hedge funds be made public. The recommended disclosures included value at risk and the results of stress tests.[1] However, this recommendation was not implemented. Without such information, it is not possible to identify building systemic risk in the hedge fund industry.

Lack of Appropriate Margin in Derivatives Trades

The LTCM experience illustrates the importance of imposing appropriate margin requirements on derivatives trades. Had the derivatives trades been centrally cleared by an organization that enforced appropriate margin requirements, the LTCM debacle might never have occurred. At the time, there were no regulations on the margins required for derivatives trades. Increased market discipline following the LTCM failure appears to have resulted in more-sensible margin requirements, but, absent regulation, the possibility remains that counterparties might once again become lax in the imposition of margin requirements.

Runs on Prime Brokers

Hedge fund runs on investment banks contributed to the financial crisis, illustrating the vulnerability of prime brokers to withdrawals by their hedge fund customers and the importance of maintaining sufficient cash and liquid assets to weather them. Vulnerability to such runs will only make them more likely. One might argue that the solution is for banks to maintain a strong balance sheet, but economic modeling has shown how banks can be subject to runs even if many depositors know that negative information about the bank is inaccurate.[2] And the solution to preventing bank runs—the establishment of the FDIC—is not a feasible solution for prime brokers. There is thus a public interest in reducing incentives for hedge funds to withdraw assets from prime

---

[1]   PWG, 1999, p. 33.

[2]   Diamond, 2007, p. 197.

brokers at the first hint of trouble. The crisis demonstrates the importance of segregating hedge fund assets from the prime broker's parent organization. Without such segregation, even a remote possibility of insolvency can lead to hedge fund withdrawals, increasing the probability of insolvency in a self-reinforcing cycle.

Short Selling

Although there is little evidence that short selling by hedge funds was a significant contributor to the financial crisis, some researchers and industry participants remain concerned about opportunistic short selling. Concern remains that this opportunistic short selling by a large hedge fund or by multiple hedge funds can result in an unjustified fall in stock prices or can cause a decline in the real value of a firm. The decline might be so rapid that there is no opportunity for the firm to dispel rumors about its financial health or for investors to provide additional capital before the firm collapses. Such collapses can pose a risk to the financial system, as well as reduce the level of economic activity.

Compromised Risk-Management Incentives

The failure of the Bear Stearns hedge funds raises concerns about embedding hedge funds within larger financial institutions. In the case of Bear Stearns, reputational concerns led it to bail out the hedge funds, creating additional strain on a systemically important institution. The Bear Stearns experience more generally underscores the dangers of hedge funds that are directly or indirectly subsidized by taxpayers. Such subsidies may arise from a parent organization's access to the Federal Reserve discount window or from implicit guarantees that result when regulators deem a fund or parent organization too big to fail. In such situations, hedge fund managers no longer bear the full consequences of their investment decisions, and inadequate risk management can result. These inadequate risk-management incentives can result in the buildup of systemic risk if the financial institution is highly interconnected with the rest of the financial system.

Lack of Portfolio Liquidity and Excessive Leverage

It is difficult to come to strong conclusions about the extent to which hedge fund deleveraging contributed to the financial crisis, but the potential remains for hedge fund deleveraging to cause weaknesses in the financial system.

Although hedge funds did not appear to be highly leveraged on the whole during the financial crisis, the reduction of the credit provided to hedge funds by prime brokers and investor withdrawals during the crisis underscore the importance of limiting leverage. If margin requirements on credit are very low (and thus leverage high), then modest credit reductions can precipitate large asset sales, potentially precipitating a price downdraft. A similar argument holds for the impact of investor withdrawals in a highly leveraged environment. Leverage discipline is thus important in moderating the potential systemic risk posed by hedge funds through both the market and credit channels.

Perhaps of greater concern than high leverage is the potential for the decreased liquidity of hedge fund investments. The financial crisis caused both hedge fund managers and investors to reassess assumptions made on the liquidity of their investments. It also caused both to reassess the value they place on liquidity and the importance of financing that enables hedge funds to avoid selling assets at distressed prices. Concern about the liquidity of hedge fund portfolios is also driven by research that indicates the increasing correlation of returns across the industry. In his 2008 congressional testimony, Andrew Lo, professor at the Massachusetts Institute of Technology Sloan School of Management, notes,

> Greater illiquidity risk and leverage as hedge funds undertook more exotic investments using greater leverage to boost their returns, and . . . greater correlation among different hedge fund strategies, particularly with respect to losses.

Lo is also concerned about hedge fund strategies that "can cause market dislocation in crowded markets with participants that are not

fully aware of or prepared for the crowdedness of their investments."[3]
Using monthly data on hedge fund returns between 1977 and 2004,
Chan, Getmansky, Hass, and Lo find that one proxy for the illiquidity of hedge fund portfolios has been increasing.[4] Research by Boyson,
Stahel, and Stulz suggests that financial shocks can affect hedge funds
broadly, aggravating a crisis. They conclude that large changes in liquidity (either of assets themselves or in the funding available to hedge
funds—so-called funding liquidity) help explain the result.[5]

The implication of this research and events during the financial crisis is that, from a systemic-risk point of view, it is increasingly
important to pay attention to the liquidity of hedge fund investments.
It is also important to realize that, even if no one hedge fund may be
large enough to pose a systemic risk to the financial system, negative
shocks can affect hedge funds as a group, with ramifications cascading
through the economy.[6] Thus, it may not be enough to pay attention to
only the largest hedge funds when considering systemic risk. The consequence for regulators concerned about financial-system stability is
that the financial condition of the entire hedge fund industry, not just
of the largest funds, is relevant.

During the crisis, there was no direct regulation of hedge fund
leverage and liquidity. Rather, control of leverage and liquidity relied
on market discipline and indirect regulation through banks and prime
brokers that were, in turn, overseen by regulators. As discussed in
Chapter Three, the LTCM experience demonstrates that the oversight
of hedge funds by prime brokers and other counterparties can break
down, while the track record in the ensuing years illustrates that this

---

[3] Lo, 2008, p. 10.

[4] Chan et al. use the serial correlation in a fund's monthly returns as proxy for lack of
liquidity (2006, pp. 60, 63).

[5] When reviewing the association between returns over time for different hedge fund
investment strategies, Boyson, Stahel, and Stulz (2010) find that low returns occur more
often at the same time than would occur by chance.

[6] In a 2012 *Financial Times* article, Authers argues that too many hedge funds are making
the same bet, with the result that trades are overcrowded and returns are looking ever more
like the stock market itself (Authers, 2012).

type of indirect regulation can work. However, there is no guarantee that market discipline and indirect regulation will remain strong. Oversight by prime brokers and other creditors may loosen as memories of LTCM and the financial crisis recede.

Financial Reforms That Address Hedge Fund Contributions to Systemic Risk

How can the potential threats discussed here that hedge funds pose to the financial system be addressed? Many of the financial reforms currently in various stages of discussion and enactment aim to address exactly these threats. We examine in some detail how the Dodd-Frank Wall Street Reform and Consumer Protection Act, which was enacted in the aftermath of the financial crisis, and other recent reforms address the six areas identified above.[7]

Dodd-Frank seeks to "promote the financial stability of the United States" with a far-reaching set of provisions, many of which affect hedge funds.[8] Our objective is not to provide a detailed assessment of the efficacy of the recent reforms because many are still in progress but rather to provide observations on whether key issues are being addressed and to identify the gaps that remain. For convenience, the sections of Dodd-Frank and the other regulations that address the areas of concern are summarized in the appendix.

Reforms That Address Lack of Information on Hedge Funds

Dodd-Frank contains several provisions that are aimed at improving the information available on the activities of hedge funds. This information might help regulators determine the circumstances under which hedge funds pose systemic risks.

---

[7]   We use *address* to mean that an effort is being made to tackle or solve a problem. We do not use it to signal that the problem has been fixed or even lessened by the regulatory reform or the strength of enforcement.

[8]   U.S. Senate, 2010.

Registration Requirements for Investment Advisers

Dodd-Frank requires hedge fund advisers with $150 million or more in AUM to register with the SEC.[9] Dodd-Frank requires investment advisers to register by July 21, 2011, although the SEC has extended the deadline to March 30, 2012. The SEC estimates that approximately 750 private-fund advisers that did not register prior to Dodd-Frank will be required to register by the March deadline.[10] Figure 2.5 in Chapter Two indicates that, post–Dodd-Frank, between 71 percent and 93 percent of the AUM by the hedge fund industry will be managed by advisers required to register with the SEC.[11] An adviser that is not registered with the SEC is required to register with the state in which it has its principal office, if required by the laws of that state.[12] Even though an estimated additional 750 hedge fund advisers will register with the SEC, the total number of SEC-registered advisers (including those not considered hedge fund advisers) will probably decrease. Other changes in the registration requirements mandated by Dodd-Frank will result in more than 750 registered advisers (not all of which necessarily advise hedge funds) to transfer registration from the SEC to the states.[13]

The act also exempts foreign hedge fund advisers, defining a *foreign adviser* as an adviser that has no place of business in the United

---

[9] Dodd-Frank, §§403, 408.

[10] According to SEC staff, 2,761 advisers that advise only private funds or private funds and other types of clients were registered as of April 1, 2011 (GAO, 2011, p. 8).

[11] Seventy-one percent is the sum of the percentages of industry-wide AUM in Figure 2.5 in Chapter Two for funds with more than $500 million under management. Adding the 22 percent for funds with between $100 million and $500 million in AUM increases the total to 93 percent.

[12] GAO, 2011, pp. 6–8. Dodd-Frank does not change preexisting requirements that an investment adviser that is not registered with federal regulators may be required to register as an adviser with one or more state securities authorities (SEC, 2011a, fn. 24).

[13] Dodd-Frank raises the threshold under which hedge funds must register with states instead of with the SEC. Post–Dodd-Frank hedge funds that manage less than or equal to $100 million cannot register with the SEC, up from $25 million prior to Dodd-Frank. The SEC estimates that about 3,200 of the 11,500 advisers registered as of 2011 will switch from SEC to state registration (SEC, 2011b, p. 9).

States and has less than $25 million under management from U.S. investors—or a higher cutoff as determined by the SEC.[14]

Recordkeeping and Reporting Requirements

Dodd-Frank allows the SEC to impose substantial recordkeeping and reporting requirements on hedge fund advisers.[15] The act permits the SEC to require registered investment advisers to maintain records necessary for the assessment of systemic risk by the Financial Stability Oversight Council (FSOC) and to make such records available to the FSOC. The following information is required to be maintained:

- the amount of AUM
- the use of leverage, including off-balance-sheet leverage
- counterparty credit risk exposure
- trading and investment positions
- asset-valuation policies and practices
- types of assets held
- side arrangements and side letters that are entered into with a subset of investors in a fund
- trading practices
- any other information that the SEC, in consultation with the FSOC, deems necessary.[16]

Dodd-Frank also requires investment advisers exempt from registration to maintain such records and provide reports as deemed necessary by the SEC.[17] The SEC and the U.S. Commodity Futures Trading Commission (CFTC) recently adopted joint rules that establish detailed reporting requirements for hedge fund advisers.[18] Under the

---

[14] Dodd-Frank, §403.

[15] For the purposes of the regulation, records of the funds managed by the adviser are considered records of the investment adviser (§404).

[16] Dodd-Frank, §404.

[17] Dodd-Frank, §408. The FSOC can require reports from *any* financial company for the purpose of assessing risk to U.S. financial stability (Davis Polk and Wardwell, 2010, p. 2).

[18] SEC, 2012.

rule, an adviser is required to file Form PF on an annual basis if it manages between $150 million and $1.5 billion across all its funds and on a quarterly basis if it manages more than $1.5 billion. For advisers reporting on a quarterly basis, the rule requires a great deal of detail on their funds' positions.[19]

The information supplied to the SEC will remain confidential. Under Dodd-Frank, the SEC may not be compelled to disclose information required to be filed with the SEC, except under special circumstances (for example, pursuant to the order of a federal court in an action brought by the United States or the SEC) (§404).

Section 929X of Dodd-Frank imposes additional reporting requirements on short sales, which may provide additional insight into hedge fund operations. The act requires the SEC to promulgate rules providing for public disclosure of the name of the issuer and the amount of short sales for each security on a monthly basis (§929X[a]).

Enhanced Examination Authority

Dodd-Frank directs the SEC to conduct periodic inspections of the records that the hedge fund adviser is required to maintain and any additional examinations that the SEC deems necessary for the assessment of systemic risk (§404).

Data Repository for Swaps

As is described later in this chapter, Dodd-Frank creates an ambitious new regulatory system for derivatives markets. As can be seen in Table 2.1 in Chapter Two, hedge funds are active participants in derivatives markets, and their operations will be affected by the forthcoming regulations. Under the new regulatory system, all swaps (a type of derivatives trade) must be reported to a registered swap data repository (§727).[20] The requirement increases the information available on hedge fund activities and can, in principle, allow regulators to better assess the systemic risk posed by hedge funds.

---

[19] SEC, 2012. Form PF is available at SEC, undated (b).

[20] All swaps, whether or not cleared through a central clearing facility (described later in this chapter) must be reported.

Removal of Barriers to Public Disclosures by Hedge Funds

Restrictions on general solicitations and general advertising have discouraged hedge funds from providing information to the public on their strategies, operations, and returns. Congress recently instructed the SEC to remove these restrictions in the Jumpstart Our Business Startups (JOBS) Act, which was signed into law on April 5, 2012. The restrictions will now no longer apply as long as the securities are sold only to accredited investors. Hedge funds will be required to take reasonable steps to verify that their investors are accredited investors, using such methods as determined by the SEC.[21]

Observations on Reforms That Address Lack of Information on Hedge Funds

Although a substantial number of hedge fund advisers were voluntarily registered prior to Dodd-Frank, particularly the managers of larger funds, Dodd-Frank will increase the number of hedge fund advisers registered. The percentage of hedge fund assets managed by registered advisers will be substantial. The act will allow the SEC to collect a wide range of information relevant to assessing the systemic risk posed by hedge funds. The swap data repository is also a potentially valuable source of information on hedge fund operations. In addition, hedge funds will no longer have to be so cautious about providing information on their operations to the public.

The information provisions of the act go a long way toward filling long-standing gaps in knowledge about the activities of hedge funds, although the exemption granted to foreign hedge fund advisers leaves a potentially important gap.[22] It is not clear how the United States could have jurisdiction over such advisers, but the fact remains that the hedge fund industry is a global industry. Without information on the overall industry, it may be difficult to assess the systemic risk posed by hedge funds. Many foreign jurisdictions are imposing reporting requirements similar to those in the United States, and the resulting information

---

[21] Pub. L. 112-106, §201.

[22] Recall from Chapter Two that 24 percent of hedge fund advisers are based outside the United States.

may improve understanding about the systemic risk posed by hedge funds globally as long as the information is comparable and shared among regulators.[23]

Although the new information may be of substantial value to systemic-risk regulators, it comes at a cost. First, there will be some cost of complying with the regulations. According to a law firm that serves the hedge fund industry, Form PF requires a substantial amount of detail from the larger funds, and many funds will face a significant reporting burden.[24] A hedge fund expert with whom we spoke thought that complying with Form PF would be very labor intensive. Others in the industry were concerned about the costs of SEC inspections and the opened-ended provisions in Dodd-Frank that allow any additional examinations and data calls at the discretion of the SEC. Of potential concern are costs that create barriers to entry into the industry. However, only large hedge fund advisers (those with more than $1.5 billion in AUM) are required to complete the more complex portion of the form. The reporting requirements thus do not appear to create much in the way of entry barriers. Costly reporting and examination requirements create incentives for hedge fund managers to move to jurisdictions with less onerous requirements, frustrating the goals of Dodd-Frank. As discussed previously, however, other jurisdictions are also increasing reporting requirements, which may mean that there is little advantage to switching jurisdictions.[25]

A second type of cost associated with requirements to provide more information to regulators is the risk such disclosures pose for data confidentiality. Hedge funds are extremely concerned about keeping the specifics of their investment strategies confidential. An investment strategy is easily copied, and release of sensitive information can

---

[23] For example, see "Directive 2011/61/EU of the European Parliament and of the Council of 8 June 2011 on Alternative Investment Fund Managers and Amending Directives 2003/41/EC and 2009/65/EC and Regulations (EC) No 1060/2009 and (EU) No 1095/2010," 2011.

[24] Mallon, undated.

[25] Recall that foreign advisers must still register and report if they manage more than $25 million in assets from U.S. investors. Thus, if a hedge fund adviser wants access to any sizable amount of assets from U.S. investors, it will have to register in the United States.

quickly destroy a hedge fund's business model.[26] Failure to protect sensitive information can reduce the incentives for funds to enter or remain in the business, limiting the benefits that they provide to the financial system.

How useful the information provided by hedge funds will be in monitoring and reducing systemic risk is unclear. It is not clear that the information provided by hedge funds will be sufficiently current to inform real-time monitoring of systemic risk or whether it is even feasible to aggregate vast amounts of information quickly enough and act on it to prevent a systemic event. Hedge fund positions can change rapidly, and data that are even just a few weeks old may be of little relevance in assessing current risk. It remains to be seen whether even the quarterly information required of the largest funds will be adequate to identify emerging systemic risks. And it remains unclear what regulatory authorities would be able to do even if such emerging risks were identified in a timely fashion.[27]

Reforms That Address Lack of Appropriate Margin in Derivatives Trades

Dodd-Frank overhauls the market for swaps. Swaps include CDSs, interest-rate swaps, and total return swaps.[28] Title VII of the act requires mandatory clearing of certain swaps through regulated derivatives clearing organizations and defines and regulates a new category of financial-market actors called major swap participants. Some hedge funds may be classified as major swap participants.

---

[26] Fears about the release of confidential position information were confirmed when Senator Bernie Sanders sent information on oil positions collected by the CFTC to a *Wall Street Journal* reporter in June 2011 (Lynch, 2011).

[27] One regulatory staffer with whom we spoke wondered what type of action could be taken to reduce, for example, investment in an overheated sector. Public statements might trigger rapid deleveraging, while communications with a few firms would be viewed as playing favorites.

[28] Dodd-Frank, §721. Dodd-Frank categorizes the derivatives within its scope as either swaps or securities-based swaps, with the distinction based in part on whether the swap will be regulated by the CFTC or the SEC. For the purposes of our discussion, we do not distinguish between the different types of swaps because many of the act's provisions are the same for both types of swaps (Davis Polk and Wardwell, 2010, p. 53).

Dodd-Frank directs the CFTC and the SEC to determine which types of swaps must be centrally cleared (cleared swaps), and swap participants must then submit such swaps to a derivatives clearing organization.[29] The intent was for swaps that were of a standard form to be centrally cleared while OTC trades would still be available for swaps that are tailored to unique situations. Section 725 of the act details core principles with which a derivatives clearing organization must comply. Among them are risk-management principles that require the derivatives clearing organization to establish margin and other requirements that protect it from defaults by swap participants.

To reduce credit risk for swaps that are not centrally cleared (uncleared swaps), the act begins by defining major swap participants. A major swap participant is an entity that meets at least one of the following criteria:

- It maintains a substantial position in swaps.
- Its outstanding swaps create substantial counterparty exposure that could have serious adverse effects on the financial stability of the U.S. banking system or financial markets.
- It is a financial entity that is highly leveraged, is not subject to capital requirements established by the appropriate federal banking agency, and maintains a substantial position in outstanding swaps.[30]

Positions that are held for hedging or mitigation of commercial risk are excluded when determining whether an entity is a major swap participant.[31]

The act gives the CFTC and the SEC authority to define the key terms in the definition of a major swap participant (e.g., *substantial position, highly leveraged, commercial risk*), and, in December 2010, the

---

[29] Dodd-Frank, §723.

[30] Dodd-Frank, §721(a)(33)(A).

[31] Dodd-Frank, §721(a)(33)(A).

two agencies jointly issued a proposed rule for the definitions of these terms.[32]

Dodd-Frank directs the CFTC and the SEC to require minimum initial and variation margin requirements on uncleared swaps and to impose minimum capital requirements on major swap participants.[33] The capital requirements have prompted opposition from industry advocates. A leading hedge fund industry association, MFA, argues that it is inappropriate to impose capital requirements on hedge funds that are designated major swap participants because hedge funds do not hold capital. Rather, it submits, hedge funds manage assets on behalf of their investors. MFA argues that regulators should count the margin posted by a hedge fund toward any capital requirement to which it is subject.[34]

Dodd-Frank also requires swap participants to trade all cleared swaps on an exchange or a swap execution facility unless no exchange or swap execution facility makes the swap available for trading.[35]

In the year following Dodd-Frank's enactment, the CFTC and the SEC issued more than 80 proposed rules for new derivatives regulation, clearing, and oversight.[36] Although the rulemaking process is progressing, important aspects of the new derivatives regulatory structure remain uncertain. It remains to be seen, for example, what percentage of swaps is required to be centrally cleared and how many hedge funds will be classified as major swap participants.

Observations on Reforms That Address Derivatives Markets

The wide-ranging changes that Dodd-Frank authorizes in derivatives markets could, in principle, prevent a repeat of the LTCM fiasco. Initial and variation margin are now required unless the swap has been exempted by the CFTC or the SEC, reducing the likelihood that a hedge fund is able to take on tremendous risk without posting assets to

---

[32] CFTC and SEC, 2010.

[33] Dodd-Frank, §731.

[34] MFA, 2011, p. 7.

[35] Dodd-Frank, §723.

[36] PricewaterhouseCoopers, 2011, p. 8.

cover the possibility of loss. However, the regulatory authorities have a great deal of discretion in implementing the regulations, and the efficacy of the regulations remains to be seen. Our analysis suggests that market forces had already reduced the chance that another LTCM could occur, but the new regulations on derivatives markets can provide some insurance against the short memories or shortsightedness that can relax standards.[37]

Reforms That Address Hedge Fund Runs on Prime Brokers

Dodd-Frank protects the margin that hedge funds post with brokers and dealers as collateral for their derivatives positions. Section 724 requires the parties that accept the money used to provide margin, guarantee, or otherwise secure a swap through a derivatives clearing organization (cleared swaps) to be registered as futures commission merchants (FCMs). It then requires all FCMs

- to treat all such money, security, and property as belonging to the swap customer
- to separately account for and not commingle the customer's funds with the FCM's funds.

The CFTC has recently begun rulemaking on this provision of the act and is considering four different approaches for segregating the collateral posted on cleared swaps.[38]

Section 724 also contains requirements regarding the segregation of assets for uncleared swaps. A swap dealer or major swap participant must notify a party wanting to enter a swap at the beginning of the swap transaction that it has the right to require segregation of funds or other property used to provide margin or otherwise secure its obligations as a counterparty. If the party so requests, the swap dealer or

---

[37] Dodd-Frank can also reduce systemic risk in the derivatives markets created by actors other than hedge funds. For example, the margin requirements could also reduce the likelihood of a repeat of the AIG meltdown. AIG was not required to post initial margin on its CDSs (MFA, 2010, p. 5). The focus of this report, however, is on the systemic risk posed by hedge funds.

[38] Kaswell, 2011, p. 6.

major swap participant must keep the party's assets in an account separate from the assets and other interests of the swap dealer or major swap
participant. This provision prevents the swap dealer or major swap participant from using customer assets to provide margin, guarantee, or
otherwise secure any of its own trades.

Dodd-Frank also contains provisions that affect the process for
liquidating insolvent companies.[39] The new liquidation authority can
apply to any financial company, subject to a two-thirds vote by the
Federal Reserve Board of Governors and two-thirds vote of the FDIC
board or the SEC, depending on which organization is the primary
regulator of the insolvent company.[40] Certain findings by the Secretary
of the Treasury, in consultation with the President, are also required.
According to one analysis, these requirements create high procedural
hurdles and create a presumption against applying these new provisions
in a particular bankruptcy case.[41] If an insolvent company is determined to be a company covered by the provisions of the act, the FDIC
becomes the receiver. The act contains some provisions regarding how
customer assets at covered insolvent companies would be treated. Section 205 directs the FDIC to discharge all obligations relating to customer assets in a manner that is at least as beneficial to the customer
as would have been the case if the distribution were done under the
Securities Investor and Protection Act of 1970.[42]

Observations on Reforms That Address Hedge Fund Runs on Prime Brokers

Dodd-Frank provides protections that will reduce the incentives for
hedge funds to withdraw funds from their prime brokers at the first
sign of trouble. Money used for margins or to otherwise guarantee
swap positions will not be commingled with the broker's funds. Like
the establishment of deposit insurance following the bank runs of the

---

[39] Title II.

[40] Dodd-Frank, §203.

[41] Davis Polk and Wardwell, 2010, p. 23.

[42] Pub. L. 91-598.

Great Depression, these provisions will reduce the susceptibility of banks to runs by nervous hedge funds.[43]

The central clearing requirement for derivatives should also increase hedge fund confidence in the financial stability of prime brokers. With central clearing, both hedge funds and the banks that sponsor prime brokers will have to post margin, reducing the chance that banks will become overextended.

The new liquidation authority for financial companies appears aimed in part at protecting the property of the customers of broker-dealers during bankruptcy proceedings. Further research is needed to understand how the FDIC plans to implement its new responsibilities and what the impact on hedge fund assets held at an insolvent financial institution would be. Uncertainty also remains over whether authority will be exercised in the face of a particular insolvency. Because FDIC liquidation must be approved by the multiple governing boards, approval will be on a case-by-case basis, and the proclivity to grant FDIC jurisdiction may vary over time.

Market responses have also reduced the susceptibility of prime brokers to hedge fund runs and reinforce the provisions of Dodd-Frank. Many funds now insist that prime brokers agree not to use hedge fund assets to borrow or back their own positions (a process known as rehypothecation). The agreements by hedge funds and prime brokers also stipulate that hedge fund cash must be held in separate accounts.[44]

Reforms That Address Short Selling

In response to the effects of concentrated short selling in 1937, the SEC adopted the now-defunct Rule 10a-1 to restrict short selling in a declining market. Known as the uptick rule, Rule 10a-1 provided that, subject to certain exceptions, a listed security could be sold short (1) at a price above the price of the immediately preceding sales or (2) at the

---

[43] Concerns will likely remain, however, about how well the new provisions will be enforced. The 2011 bankruptcy of MF Global Holdings, a brokerage firm that specialized in futures and derivatives trades, provide a cautionary example. MF Global Holdings apparently violated preexisting prohibitions on using customer funds for its own high-risk investments in European sovereign debt ("MF Global Holdings Ltd.," 2012).

[44] Keoun, 2011.

last sale price if it was higher than the last different price.[45] The central provisions of the uptick rule remained unchanged for nearly 70 years. In 2004, the SEC created a pilot program to assess whether changes in the uptick rule were appropriate given the market conditions and market practices at that time. Informed by the results of the pilot, the SEC eliminated the uptick rule, effective July 3, 2007. Extreme market volatility during the financial crisis and calls for reinstatement of the uptick rules from investors and securities issuers alike led the SEC to adopt four emergency orders that placed restrictions on short sales at various times during 2008, including a ban on short selling for approximately 1,000 mainly financial stocks for three weeks in September 2008. Subsequent to the financial crisis, the SEC adopted Rule 201, a permanent rule on short selling that was adopted February 24, 2010 (compliance with the rule was required on November 10, 2010).

Rule 201 contains both a circuit breaker and an alternative uptick rule. The circuit breaker is triggered for a security when its price falls 10 percent or more from the prior day's closing. Once the circuit breaker has been triggered, an uptick rule would apply to short sales for that security for the remainder of the day, as well as the following day. The uptick rule allows short selling only if the price of the security is above the current national best bid or the last sale price.[46] Rule 201 applies to all equity securities that are listed on a national securities exchange, whether traded on an exchange or in the OTC market.

In addition to reinstating a modified uptick rule, the SEC has strengthened prohibitions on naked short selling. In 2005, the SEC adopted Regulation SHO to address persistent failures to deliver stock on the trade settlement date and to eliminate potentially abusive naked short selling. During the financial crises, the SEC became concerned that short sellers were not complying with the 2005 regulation, and, in response, it adopted Rule 10b-21 on September 17, 2008. The naked short-selling antifraud rule requires a short seller and its broker or dealer to deliver securities by the close of business on the settlement

---

[45] SEC, 2010a, p. 15.

[46] SEC, 2010a, p. 56. The best bid is the best available bid price while selling securities.

date (which is three days after the sale transaction date).[47] If a short sale violates the closeout requirement, then the broker or dealer acting on the short seller's behalf will be prohibited from selling short in the same security unless the shares are preborrowed.

Section 929X of Dodd-Frank imposes some additional reforms on short sales. The act requires the SEC to promulgate rules providing for public disclosure of the name of the issuer and the amount of short sales for each security on a monthly basis.[48] The act reaffirms that the manipulative short sale of any security is unlawful, and it is up to the SEC to define *manipulative short selling*, develop appropriate enforcement mechanisms, and establish penalties for violations.[49] Dodd-Frank also allows a security owner to instruct brokers and dealers that its securities are not to be used in connection with short sales.[50] Finally, §417 of the act requires the SEC to conduct studies on the frequency with which short sellers fail to deliver securities and the desirability of requiring short sales to be publicly reported in real time.

Observations on Reforms That Address Short Sales

The rules adopted by the SEC over the past three years and the requirements in Dodd-Frank have fundamentally altered the market for short sales. The ability of short sales to push down prices in a falling market has been limited. However, it remains to be seen whether a 10-percent trigger and the one to two days the uptick rule is in place following the trigger's pulling appropriately balance the costs and benefits of restricting short sales. For example, the restrictions on short selling may provide more time for sovereign wealth funds and other large investors to make bids that allow a firm under severe financial pressure to survive. Conversely, it could turn out that the 10-percent trigger and the one- or two-day hiatus are not enough to make much difference in the

---

[47] SEC, 2008c.

[48] Dodd-Frank, §929X(a).

[49] Dodd-Frank, §929(b). Section 10 of the Securities Exchange Act of 1934 (48 Stat. 881) outlaws price manipulation on all sales or purchases of securities and applies whether the sales or purchases are short or long.

[50] Dodd-Frank, §929X(c).

ability of short selling to push prices below levels warranted by company fundamentals. For example, Misra, Lagi, and Bar-Yam note that a 10-percent trigger would not have stopped what they consider to be a bear raid on Citigroup in the fall of 2007.[51] Experience in a variety of market conditions will be needed before the effectiveness of the new rules can be assessed.

Although public disclosure of short sales may make it easier to detect and deter opportunistic short selling, public disclosure rules may also reduce the benefits to markets and investors of short selling. According to a study by Oliver Wyman, public disclosure reduces investors' willingness to engage in short selling.[52] Investor concerns about public disclosure include loss of proprietary intellectual capital, risk of crowded trades as other investors copy the strategy, increased exposure to short squeezes, reduced willingness of corporate management to cooperate with analysts whose funds are known to short the company's stocks, and the risk that short positions will generate political or public opinion backlash.[53] Following an analysis of short-sale disclosure requirements in the United Kingdom during the financial crisis, Oliver Wyman concludes that short-sale disclosure requirements reduce short sellers' participation in equity markets by 20 to 25 percent and negatively affected several measures of market efficiency, including bid-ask spreads, market volatility, and trading volume.[54] An industry observer with whom we spoke observed that the disclosure requirements in the UK prompted hedge funds there to limit short sales to an amount below the reporting limits. Careful analysis of the costs and benefits of the new regulations on short sales is warranted.

Reforms That Address Risk-Management Incentives

Dodd-Frank puts limitations on the investments that banks can make in hedge funds (these provisions are included in that part of the act

---

[51] Citigroup shares fell 9 percent on the first day of the bear run (Misra, Lagi, and Bar-Yam, 2011).

[52] Oliver Wyman is a global management consulting firm.

[53] Oliver Wyman, 2010, p. 13.

[54] Oliver Wyman, 2010, p. 5.

referred to as the *Volcker Rule*). The relevant section of the act starts with a broad prohibition: "Unless otherwise provided in this section, a banking entity shall not . . . acquire or retain any equity, partnership, or other ownership interest in or sponsor a hedge fund or a private equity fund."[55] However, the act subsequently provides conditions under which a banking entity may participate in a hedge fund.

A banking entity can organize and offer a hedge fund, can serve as a general partner or managing member of the fund, and can select or control the management of the fund subject to conditions that include the following:

- The banking entity provides bona fide trust, fiduciary, or investment advisory services, and the fund is offered only in connection with the provision of such services to persons who are customers of the banking entity.
- The banking entity does not acquire or retain an equity interest, partnership interest, or other ownership interest in the fund except for a de minimis investment.
- The banking entity does not, directly or indirectly, guarantee, assume, or otherwise insure the obligations or performance of the hedge fund or of any hedge fund in which such hedge fund invests.
- The banking entity does not share with the hedge fund for corporate, marketing, promotional, or other purposes the same name or a variation of the same name.
- No director or employee of the banking entity takes or retains an equity interest, partnership interest, or other ownership interest in the hedge fund, except for any director or employee of the banking entity who is directly engaged in providing investment advisory or other services to the hedge fund.
- The banking entity discloses to prospective and actual investors in the fund, in writing, that any losses in such hedge funds are borne solely by investors in the fund and not by the banking entity.[56]

---

[55] Dodd-Frank, §619.

[56] Dodd-Frank, §619(d)(1)(G).

A banking entity can thus run a hedge fund that is open to its customers, and a bank employee can be the investment adviser of the fund (and invest his or her personal assets in the hedge fund). However, the bank itself cannot have more than a de minimis equity stake in the hedge fund. The de minimis investment requirement allows the banking entity to provide the fund with sufficient initial capital to permit the fund to attract investors. However, the act requires that

- the banking entity's ownership interest in the fund be 3 percent or less no later than one year after the fund's establishment, but the Federal Reserve retains the authority to extend the deadline to three years
- the interest of the banking entity in all funds with which it is involved cannot exceed 3 percent of its tier 1 capital.[57]

The limitation on ownership interest means that the banking industry's interest in hedge funds will be moderate. As of June 2011, the tier 1 capital of all U.S. banks totaled $1.202 trillion.[58] Restricting hedge fund investments to 3 percent of tier 1 capital would mean that bank investment would be limited to $36 billion, little more than 1 percent of the approximately $2.5 trillion of AUM by the global hedge fund industry. JPMorgan Chase, the largest U.S. bank by asset size, would be permitted to invest only $3.24 billion in all hedge funds—a small percentage of the $26 billion that was managed by JPMorgan Chase hedge funds in June 2011 (see Table 2.2 in Chapter Two).

Observations on Reforms That Address Risk-Management Incentives
By limiting the role banks can play in hedge funds, Dodd-Frank addresses one way in which hedge fund managers do not bear the full cost of risk taking. Banks will be limited in how much taxpayer-subsidized capital they can invest in hedge funds, and hedge fund managers may think it less likely that they will be rescued by taxpayer-subsidized loans. However, limiting equity stakes in hedge funds may

---

[57] Dodd-Frank, §619(d)(4). Tier 1 capital is the core capital of a bank and includes equity capital and disclosed reserves (Investopedia, 2012).

[58] "Tier 1 Capital Ratio," undated.

not eliminate the problem altogether. The central issue in avoiding future debacles like those of the Bear Stearns hedge funds is whether there is an expectation that a bank will bail out a failing hedge fund. Even if a bank has a small percentage ownership in a hedge fund, it may still feel obligated to bail out a failing fund to preserve its own reputation. It remains to be seen whether the wall erected by Dodd-Frank between hedge funds and banks is sufficiently solid. Dodd-Frank requires a bank to notify investors that hedge fund losses are borne solely by the investors in the fund and not by the bank and that the bank does not directly or indirectly guarantee the performance of the fund.[59] But a bank could still bail out a hedge fund with taxpayer-subsidized capital if it so chooses. Even if the hedge fund and the bank have very different names and the bank owns a small share of the equity capital, the hedge fund's investors may be bank customers, and the bank may feel that its brand would be damaged if it does not bail out a failing fund.

Dodd-Frank's restrictions on hedge fund investments apply only to U.S. banks and their affiliates and subsidiaries. Hedge funds may be housed in foreign institutions that have access to subsidized credit or be considered too big to fail in their home jurisdictions, potentially compromising the risk-management incentives of hedge fund advisers. Competition among hedge funds may encourage relaxation of risk management at other hedge funds. Further work is needed to understand the extent to which regulations in other countries could allow hedge funds to externalize their losses and how any consequent relaxation of risk-management practices by some funds would affect the industry as whole.[60]

---

[59] In addition, §23B of the Federal Reserve Act prohibits banks from engaging in transactions with affiliates that are not on terms substantially the same as for comparable transactions with nonaffiliated companies (12 U.S.C. 371c-1).

[60] For example, review of restrictions in other countries on the investments that banks can make in U.S. hedge funds is warranted.

Reforms That Address the Liquidity and Leverage of Hedge Fund Portfolios

The Dodd-Frank Act contains provisions that address the direct, indirect, and self-regulation of hedge funds. *Direct regulation* refers to the oversight and regulation of hedge funds by federal regulators. *Indirect regulation* refers to the requirements on hedge fund operations imposed by prime brokers that are, in turn, directly regulated by federal regulators. *Self-regulation* refers to oversight and enforcement by a private organization. Government regulators might delegate some of their regulatory authorities to such a self-regulatory organization (SRO).

Direct Regulation of Hedge Funds

Regulation of Systemically Important Nonbank Financial Companies

Dodd-Frank allows the FSOC to determine that a nonbank financial company, including a hedge fund, could pose a substantial threat to the financial stability of the United States.[61] Once designated, these SINBFCs are subject to regulation by the Federal Reserve. The FSOC can also recommend that the Federal Reserve strengthen the prudential standards on a particular SINBFC beyond those typically imposed.

In April 2012, the FSOC issued a final rule describing the process it will follow to designate a nonbank financial company as systemically important. The FSOC may designate a nonbank financial company as systemically important if the FSOC determines that "'material financial distress' at the company could pose a threat to U.S. financial stability" or

> the nature, scope, size, scale, concentration, interconnectedness, or mix of the activities of the nonbank financial company's business practices, conduct, or operations could pose a threat to U.S. financial stability, regardless of whether the nonbank financial company is experiencing financial distress.[62]

---

[61] Dodd-Frank, §113.

[62] FSOC, 2012, p. 78. According to the FSOC, material financial distress exists when a nonbank financial company is in imminent danger of insolvency or defaulting on its financial obligations.

The rule sets up a three-stage process of increasingly in-depth evaluation and analysis leading up to proposed determination as an SINBFC. Firms that meet the criteria for one stage pass on to the next stage. A nonbank financial institution will pass through stage 1 if its total consolidated assets total $50 billion or more *and* it meets or exceeds one of the following thresholds:

- $30 billion in gross notional CDSs
- $3.5 billion in derivatives liabilities
- $20 billion in total debt outstanding
- a leverage ratio of 15 to 1
- a ratio of total debt outstanding with maturity of less than 12 months to total consolidated assets of 0.1.[63]

Importantly, the FSOC may consider the aggregate risks posed by separate hedge funds that are managed by the same adviser, particularly if the funds' investments are identical or highly similar.

In stage 2, the FSOC will analyze the potential threat that each of the firms identified in stage 1 poses to U.S. financial stability. In contrast to the quantitative thresholds used in stage 1, the FSOC intends to evaluate the risk profile and characteristics of each individual firm based on a wide range of quantitative and qualitative industry-specific and firm-specific factors. For the firms that make it to stage 3, the FSOC will assess the systemic risk posed by the company based on information collected directly from the company, as well as the public and regulatory information used in stages 1 and 2. A nonbank firm will be designated systemically important upon a two-thirds vote of the FSOC, including an affirmative vote by the Secretary of the Treasury.

It is not clear yet how many hedge fund advisers will exceed the $50 billion threshold. Bloomberg reported what will likely be taken as an initial measure of total consolidated assets for the 50 largest hedge fund advisers that have so far registered under the SEC's new registra-

---

[63] FSOC, 2012, pp. 88–89.

tion rules.[64] Only four hedge fund advisers exceeded the $50 billion threshold. Although the list was incomplete, the Bloomberg list does suggest that the number of advisers exceeding the limit may be modest.[65] Moreover, some advisers close to the threshold may decide to shed assets in order to avoid designation. Funds identified in stage 1 may also be dropped in stage 2, particularly if the FSOC determines that some of funds managed by the investment adviser should not be aggregated because their portfolios differ significantly from those of the remaining funds.

It remains to be seen how many hedge funds the FSOC will deem systemically important. A leading hedge fund industry association concludes that applying the criteria in §113 of the act "should lead to the conclusion that it is highly unlikely that any hedge fund is systemically important at this time";[66] however, competing conclusions may well emerge.

Once a firm has been designated as an SINBFC, the act directs the Federal Reserve, either on its own or pursuant to recommendations of the FSOC, to establish prudential standards for it. The standards must include

- risk-based capital requirements and leverage limits unless the Fed, in consultation with the FSOC, determines that such requirements are not appropriate
- liquidity requirements
- overall risk-management requirements
- a resolution plan
- credit exposure report requirements.

---

[64] Weiss, 2012. Funds are ranked by regulatory AUM, which roughly reflects the equity capital of the fund multiplied by leverage. In contrast, the data in Table 2.2 in Chapter Two represent equity capital.

[65] Only three of the top ten hedge funds listed in Table 2.2 in Chapter Two are included in the Bloomberg list.

[66] MFA, 2010, p. 11.

The Fed may, but is not required to, establish

- contingent capital requirements
- enhanced public disclosure requirements
- short-term debt limits
- other standards that the Fed, on its own or pursuant to recommendations of the FSOC, determines are appropriate.[67]

The act provides specific guidance on what factors must be considered when setting standards. For example, the Fed is required to take into account any off-balance-sheet activities in calculating capital requirements, including interest-rate swaps, credit swaps, and letters of credit.[68]

Position Limits

As part of new regulations on derivatives markets, Dodd-Frank directs the CFTC to establish limits on the size of positions that may be held by any person in futures and options markets.[69] Limits are required for individual financial instruments, as well as for the "aggregate number or amount of positions in contracts based on the same underlying commodity by any person, including any group or class of traders."[70] The limits apply to physical commodities other than excluded commodities and do not apply to bona fide hedging positions. The CFTC has authority to determine limits and has the authority to exempt any commodity or class of transaction from position limits.[71] Thus, although these provisions of the act could, in principle, have a significant impact

---

[67] Dodd-Frank, §165.

[68] Dodd-Frank, §165. Section 171 of the act (the Collins Amendment) provides quantitative limits on leverage and risk-based capital ratios (see discussion in Davis Polk and Wardwell, 2010, pp. 48–49). Although SINBFCs are subject to §171, §165 also grants the Fed, in consultation with the FSOC, the authority to exempt SINBFCs from leverage limits and risk-based capital requirements.

[69] Dodd-Frank, §737.

[70] Dodd-Frank, §737.

[71] Dodd-Frank, §737(a)(7).

on at least some hedge funds, the actual impact will depend on implementation by the CFTC.

Stress Tests

The Federal Reserve must conduct annual stress tests of SINBFCs. The stress tests aim to evaluate whether a company has the capital necessary to absorb losses as a result of adverse economic conditions and are to be done under three sets of assumptions about the economic environment (baseline, adverse, and severely adverse).[72] Dodd-Frank also requires any financial company with more than $10 billion in total consolidated assets that is regulated by a primary federal financial regulatory agency to conduct an annual stress test.[73] Such a company is required to submit a report on the tests to the Fed and its primary federal financial regulatory agency and to publish a summary of the results.[74] Data are not yet available on the number of funds with more than $10 billion in total consolidated assets. Bloomberg reports that 44 exceed the $10 billion threshold, but, as discussed above, that list is incomplete.

The Federal Reserve issued a final rule on capital and stress-testing requirements for bank holding companies in November 2011.[75] Through separate rulemaking, the Fed expects that the proposal's requirements will be extended to nonbank financial companies supervised by the Fed pursuant to §113 of the Dodd-Frank Act.[76] It is not clear how the Federal Reserve will be able to act on the results of hedge fund stress tests—particularly those of hedge funds that are not considered SINBFCs.

Indirect Regulation

Many of the prime brokers used by hedge funds are parts of firms that might be designated systemically important bank holding companies.

---

[72] Dodd-Frank, §165(i).

[73] Under §2 of Dodd-Frank, the SEC is the primary federal financial regulatory agency for hedge fund advisers.

[74] Dodd-Frank, §165(i).

[75] Board of Governors of the Federal Reserve System, 2011b.

[76] Board of Governors of the Federal Reserve System, 2011a, p. 35352.

Dodd-Frank directs the Federal Reserve to establish prudential standards for such institutions that are more stringent than the standards and requirements applicable to bank holding companies that do not present similar risks to the financial stability of the United States.[77] The Federal Reserve is required to establish enhanced standards for risk-based capital, leverage, and liquidity. It is also required to establish credit exposure reporting requirements. Like SINBFCs, systemically important bank holding companies must undergo annual stress tests using different sets of assumptions.

Self-Regulation

The act requires GAO to conduct a study of the feasibility of forming an SRO to oversee hedge funds. GAO released its study in July 2011.[78] GAO found that, although establishing such an organization is feasible, doing so would require legislative action. Other hurdles identified by GAO include the start-up costs and difficulties in establishing fees and governance structures that address the needs and interests of both small and large firms.[79] GAO finds that the Financial Industry Regulatory Authority (FINRA) might provide a good model for a private-fund SRO but concludes that there would still be hurdles related to hiring and training staff because no SRO has experience in examining investment advisers for compliance.[80]

By making available additional funding and staff for examinations, GAO notes that an SRO for private-fund advisers could allow for more examinations given resource limits at the SEC. Membership fees would provide a stable source of funding for conducting oversight.

---

[77] Dodd-Frank, §165. The affected institutions would include banks that, prior to the financial crisis, were categorized as investment banks. Some of these organizations were bought by bank holding companies (for example, Merrill Lynch was bought by Bank of America). Others, including Goldman Sachs and Morgan Stanley, changed their status from investment bank to bank holding company.

[78] Dodd-Frank, §416.

[79] The report points out that the start-up costs for an SRO established in 2003, the Public Company Accounting Oversight Board, were on the order of $20 million.

[80] FINRA is an SRO that oversees securities firms. Responsibility for the regulation of securities firms ultimately lies with the SEC, but it has delegated this authority to FINRA.

The SEC, however, would still be required to oversee the SRO, adding to demands on the SEC budget. GAO also raises concerns about the potential for conflicting or inconsistent interpretations of regulations by the SRO and the SEC.

Observations on Reforms That Address the Liquidity and Leverage of Hedge Fund Portfolios

Dodd-Frank provides the framework for financial regulators to directly regulate hedge fund investment practices that contribute to systemic risk, including the establishment of liquidity and leverage requirements. The regulations implementing Dodd-Frank presume that a hedge fund adviser with less than $50 billion in consolidated assets is not an SINBFC. At its peak, LTCM's consolidated assets were on the order of $125 billion, so it would have exceeded this threshold.[81] Whether $50 billion is the appropriate threshold is open to debate, but, in any case, it seems likely that the $50 billion threshold will mean that the number of hedge fund advisers subject to direct regulation will be small or modest. Similarly, the number of hedge funds that must conduct annual stress tests is modest. Thus, it seems unlikely that direct regulation will have much impact on hedge fund liquidity.

It may well be appropriate that very few hedge funds be designated as SINBFCs. There may be few that are large enough to pose a substantial risk on their own. And a reasonable regulatory strategy is to induce large hedge funds to reduce their size so that they are not considered systemically important. However, two observations are worth making. First, having few nonbank SINBFCs means that the oversight of hedge funds will rely on market discipline and indirect regulation. Market discipline can erode, and it is difficult to see how prime brokers could effectively monitor systemic risk in some dimensions. For example, a prime broker does not appear particularly well equipped to monitor the liquidity risks posed across the hedge fund industry. Second, a firm-by-firm designation process does not address the risk of a large number of small and medium-sized firms following similar investment

---

[81]   Recall from Chapter Three that LTCM's AUM peaked at roughly $5 billion and the leverage was more than 25. LTCM grew rapidly, which does raise concern about whether there would have been adequate time to designate it as an SINBFC before it imploded.

strategies. Dodd-Frank gives financial regulators a great deal of discretion in crafting regulations, so regulations could, in principle, be crafted that address industry-wide liquidity issues.[82] However, there is no guarantee that such risks will be addressed.

Position limits authorized by the act can theoretically reduce concentration and increase the liquidity of hedge fund portfolios. However, some factors may attenuate their efficacy. First, the limits apply only to physical commodities, such as oil or natural gas, and therefore will not be able to address the illiquidity that can be created by large positions in markets for financial derivatives. Second, as with regulations on major swap participants, position limits may not be well suited to the systemic risks that result when large numbers of moderately sized hedge funds take similar positions. Third, positions that are required for bona fide hedging are excluded from limit calculations. Although such an exemption is sensible, difficulty in determining when positions are for bona fide hedging and when they are not may compromise the efficacy of position limits.[83]

In addition to position limits, Dodd-Frank authorizes limits on short-term debt for SINBFCs. Such authority would presumably allow the Fed to impose financing requirements that would reduce pressure on hedge funds to sell assets at distressed prices and contribute to a liquidity spiral. Again, however, few hedge funds may be determined to be SINBFCs.

Turning to the indirect regulation of hedge funds through prime brokers, it is too soon to tell how much more stringent the Federal Reserve's enhanced oversight of systemically important bank holding companies will be than the oversight prior to Dodd-Frank. The

---

[82] See Dodd-Frank, §120:

> The [FSOC] may provide for more stringent regulation of a financial activity . . . if the [FSOC] determines that the conduct, scope, nature, size, scale, concentration, or interconnectedness of such activity or practice could create or increase the risk of significant liquidity, credit, or other problems spreading among bank holding companies and nonbank financial companies, financial markets of the United States, or low-income, minority, or underserved communities.

[83] It should also be noted that too narrow a definition can result in limits that constrain valid hedging strategies.

enhanced standards might entail closer supervision of hedge funds by prime brokers and more-stringent limits on hedge fund leverage and liquidity. As discussed previously, the systemic risk posed by hedge funds through the credit channel is currently not a major concern. The real question is whether increased oversight by prime brokers can reduce systemic risk through the market channel. For example, will the enhanced oversight of bank holding companies translate into closer monitoring of the concentration of hedge fund positions, the alignment of debt and asset maturities, and other factors related to portfolio liquidity? Will prime brokers keep hedge fund credit to levels that will not create excessive deleveraging should prime brokers subsequently withdraw credit? It may be unrealistic to expect indirect regulation of hedge funds through prime brokers to address the liquidity risk. The fact that hedge funds often use multiple prime brokers (which, on the one hand, may reduce systemic risk through the credit channel) means that no one prime broker may have enough information to assess liquidity risk. What is more, efforts to maintain leverage discipline may diminish as memories of the last financial crisis fade.

Many issues need to be explored in assessing the advisability of delegating regulatory authority to a self-regulatory institution. Delegation of oversight and enforcement may make sense in some areas but not others. For example, delegation may work fine for data reporting. It may be less effective for limiting systemic risk through the market channel, in part because appropriate regulation of hedge fund behaviors that can affect systemic risk requires information on the overall state of the financial sector, and it is unclear that a self-regulatory institution will have access to the information required to make informed judgments.

An assessment of Dodd-Frank provisions that regulate the activities of hedge funds must also consider potential costs of such regulations. Attention should be paid to whether restrictions on leverage, liquidity, and other aspects of hedge fund operations reduce the contributions of the hedge fund industry to the financial system and the economy more broadly. These potential contributions include financial intermediation and the provision of capital to underserved sectors. Attention should also be paid to the possibility that more-stringent regulation in the United States could induce hedge funds to move to jurisdictions that have less-strict oversight than that in place even before the recent reforms. The reductions of systemic risk due to the regulations must be weighed against any reductions in hedge funds' ability to provide value to their investors and the economy more generally, as well as the costs of overseeing numerous small and medium-sized financial institutions.

The transient nature of hedge funds should also be considered in assessing the regulatory approach. Banks are typically long-lived organizations that develop robust regulatory compliance departments over time. Hedge funds, in contrast, are much more transient. A hedge fund can grow very rapidly if the investment strategy is effective but can also decrease rapidly in size or fail if the investment strategy is unsuccessful. As shown in Figure 4.1 in Chapter Four, the number of annual launches and liquidations can be a substantial proportion of the number of funds in the industry. It may be inefficient from a social point of view for a hedge fund to build an expensive regulatory compliance structure when it might be out of business in a few years; however, transience in itself does not justify lack of regulation because the rapid growth of relatively short-lived funds could lead to systemic risk.

In sum, it is not clear that the financial reforms will do much to change potential behaviors of hedge funds in terms of leverage and portfolio liquidity. Regulators will have a great deal more information about hedge fund strategies and positions, but it might be unrealistic to expect regulators to effectively use that information to reduce systemic risk. The time delays in reporting may be too great, and the hedge fund industry may move far too quickly for regulators to have any impact. For example, would the regulatory apparatus be nimble enough to detect the rapid buildup of highly leveraged bets that occurred at LTCM? Few, if any, hedge funds will be subject to direct regulation under the new regime, leaving the oversight of hedge fund leverage and liquidity to prime brokers that are, in turn, overseen by the Federal Reserve. Such oversight may not result in any meaningful restraint, particularly as memories of the financial crisis fade and the competition among prime brokers for hedge fund business intensifies. The potential thus remains for the buildup of highly leveraged, illiquid hedge fund portfolios and massive deleveraging when prime brokers withdraw credit in response to a financial shock.

Summary

Regulations being developed in the wake of the financial crisis are fundamentally changing the environment in which hedge funds operate. This sea change may seem ironic, given that, from our assessment and the analysis of others, it does not appear that hedge funds played a major role in precipitating the financial crisis. But regardless of whether the changes are warranted by the actions of hedge funds during the financial crisis, they do tackle to greater or lesser degrees the six areas of concern we have identified regarding hedge funds' potential contribution to systemic risk.

The reforms aggressively address gaps in the information available to regulators on hedge fund operations. They will provide a great deal more information about the derivatives market, a market that was at the heart of the financial crisis and in which hedge funds are major players. The reforms also aggressively address the potential for inadequate margins in derivatives trades. Absent the exemptions of major categories of derivatives in the rulemaking process, these reforms should help prevent the buildup of highly leveraged positions that can lead to the rapid failure of a large fund.

The reforms go a long way in addressing factors that can lead to hedge fund runs on prime brokers. Segregation of hedge fund assets at prime brokers and the central clearing requirements will ensure that prime brokers post appropriate margins in derivatives trades and reduce the incentives of hedge funds to withdraw funds at the first sign of trouble at their prime brokers. However, the hedge funds will still have the option to deposit funds in nonsegregated accounts at foreign subsidiaries of U.S. banks. The potential remains that hedge fund runs at these subsidiaries will weaken the parent organization.

The reforms make considerable progress in addressing the next two areas of concern, short selling and compromised risk-management incentives, but some questions remain about the effectiveness and comprehensiveness of the approach. Much more information about short sales will be available as a result of the legislation, which could deter opportunistic short selling. However, the efficacy of the new criteria for suspending short sales remains to be seen. The Volcker Rule restricting hedge fund investments by taxpayer-subsided banks can curtail one scenario in which risk-management incentives are compromised. However, it remains to be seen how the rule will be implemented. In addition, other situations that can potentially compromise risk-management incentives remain.

Perhaps the area least well addressed by the reforms is controls on portfolio liquidity and leverage. Few, if any, hedge funds will be subject to direct regulations. Position limits will not apply to the types of derivatives of greatest concern during the financial crisis, and the regulations do not address herd behavior by multiple hedge funds. Oversight of prime brokers may be more stringent, but it is difficult to see how this oversight can translate into more-effective indirect regulation of the liquidity of hedge fund portfolios. Prime brokers still have the ability to let leverage rise to levels that will cause rapid deleveraging when these prime brokers themselves have to reduce outstanding credit in response to financial shocks that affect the brokers. It is not clear that, in the end, much will have changed once all the regulations are in place for this area of concern. The potential remains for the leverage of large funds to quickly balloon and for the industry to find itself needing to sell assets in very illiquid markets when the next crisis hits.

Rulemaking for many of these regulations remains in process, and many of the critical provisions are not yet determined. As the shape of the new set of regulations becomes clearer, further work will be needed on the extent to which they reduce the systemic risks posed by hedge funds and the areas that remain to be addressed. In the concluding chapter, we identify considerations that should be kept in mind as the regulations continue to be developed and as they are evaluated.

CHAPTER SIX

Conclusion

Hedge funds are a dynamic part of the global financial system. They engage in innovative investment strategies that can improve the performance of financial markets and facilitate the flow of capital from savers to users. Although hedge funds play a useful role in the financial system, there is concern that their dynamism can contribute to system instability. Such concerns are reinforced by the lack of information about hedge fund operations and investments. The lack of information has made it easy to characterize hedge funds as villains operating in the shadows of the financial system.

From our analysis, we conclude that hedge funds have the potential to contribute to systemic risk. Although they were not a primary cause of the financial crisis, some aspects of hedge fund operations likely contributed to the crisis. The collapse of LTCM in the late 1990s also illustrates the risks they can pose to the stability of the financial system. Dodd-Frank and other reforms are addressing many aspects of hedge fund operations that can create systemic risk. However, the regulations are under development, and their effectiveness in reducing system risk will depend on what provisions are ultimately adopted and the extent to which they are enforced, which may not be known for several years.

In any case, it does appear that that there are several gaps that policymakers and regulators should address moving forward.

First, and perhaps most importantly, it would seem that the potential remains for hedge funds to build highly leveraged and illiquid portfolios. Regulators will have a great deal more information about hedge fund strategies and positions, but it may be unrealistic to expect regulators to effectively use that information to reduce systemic risk. The time delays in reporting may be too great, and the hedge fund industry may move far too quickly for regulators to have any impact. Given the size cutoffs included in recently adopted regulations, it would not be surprising if few or any hedge funds will be subject to direct regulation under the new regime, leaving the oversight of hedge fund leverage and liquidity to prime brokers that are, in turn, overseen by the Federal Reserve. Such oversight may not result in any meaningful restraint, particularly as memories of the financial crisis fade. Prime brokers are not well suited to decide from a system-wide perspective when to restrain access to credit because a single hedge fund typically uses multiple prime brokers. Prime brokers will lack a complete picture of an individual hedge fund's positions and number of counterparties. The potential remains for the buildup of highly leveraged, illiquid portfolios, and massive deleveraging when prime brokers withdraw credit in response to a financial shock.

Second, the reforms focus on the operations of the largest hedge funds, which is reasonable given that a relatively small proportion of hedge funds control a substantial fraction of industry-wide assets. However, recent research has pointed to risks created by large numbers of small or medium-sized hedge funds that pursue similar strategies. Although Dodd-Frank theoretically gives regulators authority to address such risks, it does not appear that those risks are being adequately addressed in the ensuing regulations.

Finally, the lack of coordination of regulations across national jurisdictions can frustrate efforts to reduce the systemic risks posed by hedge funds. Although U.S.-based advisers currently manage more than 75 percent of global hedge fund assets (discussed in Chapter Two), advisers and funds can easily change jurisdictions. In addition, the global financial system is tightly interconnected, and hedge fund activities in foreign jurisdictions can affect the overall hedge fund industry. Thus, it is important to coordinate regulations across jurisdictions. Coordination can reduce opportunities to avoid regulation by seeking out jurisdictions with less-stringent regulation (often referred to as regulatory arbitrage). Coordination can also prevent unnecessary duplication and inefficiencies. For example, coordination of the information requirements of the SEC's Form PF and the UK's FSA could reduce overall reporting costs, as well as ensure that comparable information is reported to both agencies.

Further analysis of the new rules as they are finalized and implemented is warranted. Additional gaps may become apparent, as well as gaps in areas that, at this point, appear well addressed. For example, particular attention should be paid to the rules affecting the trading, clearing, and reporting of derivatives because of the role derivatives played in the financial crisis and the heavy involvement of hedge funds in derivatives markets.

Our analysis does not indicate that hedge funds should be the primary concern of regulators as they strive to improve the stability of the world's financial system. However, policymakers should strive to better understand and monitor the systemic risks posed by this part of the financial system.

APPENDIX

Regulatory Reforms That Address Potential Systemic Risks Posed by Hedge Funds

Table A.1 lists and briefly describes the regulatory provisions that address the systemic risks potentially posed by hedge funds.

Table A.1
Regulatory Reforms That Address Potential Systemic Risks Posed by Hedge Funds

Bill or Regulation	Provision
Reforms that address lack of information on hedge funds	
Dodd-Frank, §403	Hedge fund managers must register with the SEC; managers with <$150 million in AUM and foreign advisers are exempt.
Dodd-Frank, §404	Hedge fund managers must keep records as determined by the SEC; even small funds must maintain records.
Dodd-Frank, §404	The SEC shall conduct periodic inspections of the records kept by hedge funds.
Dodd-Frank, §§723, 727	Many swaps must be traded on exchanges, and swaps must be reported to a registered data repository.
Dodd-Frank, §929X(a)	The SEC must promulgate rules providing for the public disclosure of short sales on a monthly basis.
JOBS Act, §201	Restrictions on general solicitations and general advertising by hedge funds are removed as long as the securities are sold only to accredited investors.

Table A.1—Continued

Bill or Regulation	Provision
Reforms that address margins in derivatives trades	
Dodd-Frank, §§721, 731	A hedge fund can be designated as a major swap participant. The SEC and the CFTC have authority to impose margin requirements on major swap participants for uncleared swaps, as well as capital requirements.
Dodd-Frank, §§723, 725	The CFTC must determine which types of swaps must be centrally cleared and requires the clearing organization to adopt margin and other requirements.
Dodd-Frank, §723	Swap participants must trade all cleared swaps on an exchange or swap execution facility unless no exchange or swap execution facility makes the swap available for trading.
Reforms that address lack of portfolio liquidity	
Direct regulation	
Dodd-Frank, §113	A hedge fund can be designated as a systemically important nonbank financial institution.
Dodd-Frank, §§165(a), 165(b)	These sections specify prudential regulations for a systemically important nonbank financial institution, including standards for leverage and liquidity.
Dodd-Frank, §165(i)	The Federal Reserve must conduct annual stress tests for systemically important nonbank financial institutions; hedge funds with assets of more than $10 billion must conduct annual stress tests on their operations.
Dodd-Frank, §737	The CFTC must establish limits on positions that may be held in futures and options markets for physical commodities (other than excluded commodities); this section does not apply to hedging positions.
Indirect regulation	
Dodd-Frank, §165	The Federal Reserve must establish heightened prudential standards for systemically important bank holding companies and must establish credit exposure reporting requirements.

Table A.1—Continued

Bill or Regulation	Provision
Self-regulation	
Dodd-Frank, §416	GAO must study feasibility of forming an SRO to oversee hedge funds.
Reforms that address risk-management incentives	
Dodd-Frank, §619	After an initial period, a bank cannot hold more than a 3% ownership in a hedge fund, and interest of a banking entity in all hedge funds combined cannot exceed 3% of its tier 1 capital.
Reforms that address opportunistic short selling	
Rule 201	This rule establishes a circuit breaker and uptick rule for short sales.
Rule 10b-21	This rule strengthens prohibitions on naked short selling.
Dodd-Frank, §417	The SEC must conduct studies on the failure to deliver on short sales and the desirability of publicly reporting short sales in real time.
Dodd-Frank, §929X(a)	The SEC must promulgate rules providing for the public disclosure of short sales on a monthly basis.
Dodd-Frank, §929X(a)	Manipulative short selling is prohibited; the SEC must enforce the prohibition.
Dodd-Frank, §929X(a)	Securities owners may deny use of their securities in connection with short sales.
Reforms that address hedge fund runs on prime brokers	
Dodd-Frank, §724	Parties that clear trades through derivatives clearing organizations must segregate customer margin from their own assets; swap dealers or major swap participants must offer to segregate margin for uncleared swaps.
Dodd-Frank, §203	There is new liquidation authority for financial companies; however, it is not clear how the new authority will affect the priority of customers in bankruptcy proceedings.

References

Agarwal, Vikas, Naveen D. Daniel, and Narayan Y. Naik, "Role of Managerial Incentives and Discretion in Hedge Fund Performance," *Journal of Finance*, Vol. 64, No. 5, October 2009, pp. 2221–2256.

"AIG Repays Bailout from N.Y. Fed," *Los Angeles Times*, June 15, 2012.

Allen, Franklin, and Douglas Gale, *Comparing Financial Systems*, Cambridge, Mass.: MIT Press, 2001.

Ang, Andrew, Sergiy Gorovyy, and Greg van Inwegen, "Hedge Fund Leverage," unpublished paper, November 29, 2010.

Authers, John, "Hedge Funds Have Grown Too Big and Need Pruning," *Financial Times*, January 30, 2012.

Barbican Consulting, "Repo Training Guide," undated. As of May 3, 2012: http://www.barbicanconsulting.co.uk/repo

Ben-David, Itzhak, Francesco Franzoni, and Rabih Moussawi, "The Behavior of Hedge Funds During Liquidity Crises," May 2010.

———, "Hedge Fund Stock Trading in the Financial Crisis of 2007–2009," *Review of Financial Studies*, Vol. 25, No. 1, 2012, pp. 1–54.

Bernanke, Ben S., "Hedge Funds and Systemic Risk," speech at the Federal Reserve Bank of Atlanta's 2006 Financial Markets Conference, Sea Island, Ga., May 16, 2006. As of July 11, 2012: http://www.federalreserve.gov/newsevents/speech/bernanke20060516a.htm

Billio, Monica, Mila Getmansky, Andrew W. Lo, and Loriana Pelizzon, "Econometric Measures of Systemic Risk in the Finance and Insurance Sectors," working paper, August 16, 2011.

Blundell-Wignall, Adrian, "An Overview of Hedge Funds and Structured Products: Issues in Leverage and Risk," *Financial Market Trends*, Vol. 2007/1, No. 92, 2007, pp. 37–57.

Board of Governors of the Federal Reserve System, "Capital Plans," proposed rule, *Federal Register*, Vol. 76, No. 117, June 17, 2011a, pp. 35351–35361. As of July 12, 2012:
http://www.gpo.gov/fdsys/pkg/FR-2011-06-17/html/2011-14831.htm

————, untitled press release, November 22, 2011b. As of July 30, 2012:
http://www.federalreserve.gov/newsevents/press/bcreg/20111122a.htm

Boehmer, Ekkehart, Charles M. Jones, and Xiaoyan Zhang, *Shackling Short Sellers: The 2008 Shorting Ban*, Lille, France: EDHEC-Risk Institute, 2009. As of July 12, 2012:
http://faculty-research.edhec.com/research/edhec-publications/2009/shackling-short-sellers-the-2008-shorting-ban-139778.kjsp

Boyson, Nicole, Jean Helwege, and Jan Jindra, "Crises, Liquidity Shocks, and Fire Sales at Financial Institutions," working paper, July 22, 2011.

Boyson, Nicole M., Christof W. Stahel, and René M. Stulz, "Hedge Fund Contagion and Liquidity Shocks," *Journal of Finance*, Vol. 65, No. 5, October 2010, pp. 1789–1816.

Brown, Gregory W., Jeremiah Green, and John R. M. Hand, "Are Hedge Funds Systemically Important?" working paper, October 7, 2010.

Brunnermeier, Markus K., and Lasse Heje Pedersen, "Market Liquidity and Funding Liquidity," *Review of Financial Studies*, Vol. 22, No. 6, 2008, pp. 2201–2238.

Burton, Katherine, "'Must Have' Hedge Funds Get Fifth of New Cash," *Bloomberg*, October 29, 2010. As of July 12, 2012:
http://www.bloomberg.com/news/2010-10-29/-must-have-hedge-funds-attract-fifth-of-new-cash-for-och-o-shea-singer.html

Centre for Hedge Fund Research, *The Value of the Hedge Fund Industry to Investors, Markets, and the Broader Economy*, KPMG International, 120401, April 2012.

CFTC—*See* U.S. Commodity Futures Trading Commission.

Chan, Nicholas, Mila Getmansky, Shane M. Haas, and Andrew W. Lo, "Do Hedge Funds Increase Systemic Risk?" *Economic Review*, Fourth Quarter 2006, pp. 49–80.

"Citadel Turning Its Sights to CMBS Lending," *Commercial Mortgage Alert*, June 25, 2010. As of July 12, 2012:
http://www.cmalert.com/headlines.php?hid=146455

"Combined Assets of Billion-Dollar Hedge Funds Nearly Flat in First Half of 2010, AR Magazine Survey Finds," *Marketwire*, September 30, 2010.

Credit Suisse Hedge Fund Index, "Dow Jones Credit Suisse Core Hedge Fund Indexes," undated. As of March 26, 2012:
http://www.hedgeindex.com/hedgeindex/en/
indexoverview.aspx?indexname=CORE&cy=USD

Davis Polk and Wardwell, *Summary of the Dodd-Frank Wall Street Reform and Consumer Protection Act, Enacted into Law on July 21, 2010*, July 21, 2010.

De Bandt, Olivier, and Philipp Hartmann, *Systemic Risk: A Survey*, Frankfurt: European Central Bank Working Paper 35, November 2000.

Diamond, Douglas, W., "Banks and Liquidity Creation: A Simple Exposition of the Diamond-Dybvig Model," *Economic Quarterly*, Vol. 93, No. 2, Spring 2007, pp. 189–200. As of July 12, 2012:
http://www.richmondfed.org/publications/research/economic_quarterly/2007/
spring/pdf/diamond.pdf

Diamond, Douglas W., and Philip H. Dybvig, "Bank Runs, Deposit Insurance, and Liquidity," *Journal of Political Economy*, Vol. 91, No. 3, June 1983, pp. 401–419.

Dichev, Ilia D., and Gwen Yu, "Higher Risk, Lower Returns: What Hedge Fund Investors Really Earn," *Journal of Financial Economics*, Vol. 100, 2011, pp. 248–263.

"Directive 2011/61/EU of the European Parliament and of the Council of 8 June 2011 on Alternative Investment Fund Managers and Amending Directives 2003/41/EC and 2009/65/EC and Regulations (EC) No 1060/2009 and (EU) No 1095/2010," July 1, 2011.

Edwards, Franklin R., "Hedge Funds and the Collapse of Long-Term Capital Management," *Journal of Economic Perspectives*, Vol. 13, No. 2, Spring 1999, pp. 189–210.

Evans, Thomas G., Stan Atkinson, and Charles H. Cho, "Hedge Fund Investing: Current Advice for Financial Advisers and Planners," *Journal of Accountancy*, February 2005. As of July 12, 2012:
http://www.journalofaccountancy.com/Issues/2005/Feb/HedgeFundInvesting.htm

Family Office Exchange, "Membership FAQs: Frequently Asked Questions," undated, referenced February 16, 2012.

FCIC—*See* Financial Crisis Inquiry Commission.

Financial Crisis Inquiry Commission, *Preliminary Staff Report: Governmental Rescues of "Too-Big-to-Fail" Financial Institutions*, August 31, 2010.

———, *The Financial Crisis Inquiry Report: Final Report of the National Commission on the Causes of the Financial and Economic Crisis in the United States*, January 2011. As of July 12, 2012:
http://www.gpo.gov/fdsys/pkg/GPO-FCIC

Financial Services Authority, *Assessing the Possible Sources of Systemic Risk from Hedge Funds: A Report on the Findings of the Hedge Fund Survey and Hedge Fund as Counterparty Survey*, London, February 2010.

——, *Assessing the Possible Sources of Systemic Risk from Hedge Funds: A Report on the Findings of the Hedge Fund Survey and Hedge Fund as Counterparty Survey*, London, February 2011.

Financial Stability Oversight Council, "Authority to Require Supervision and Regulation of Certain Nonbank Financial Companies," *Code of Federal Regulations*, Title 12, Part 1310, April 3, 2012.

"Financial Times Lexicon," undated, referenced May 2, 2012. As of July 12, 2012: http://lexicon.ft.com/

FSA—*See* Financial Services Authority.

FSOC—*See* Financial Stability Oversight Council.

GAO—*See* U.S. Government Accountability Office (before July 7, 2004, the U.S. General Accounting Office).

General rules and regulations promulgated under the Securities Act of 1933, General rules, Regulation D, Rules governing the limited offer and sale of securities without registration under the Securities Act of 1933, Rule 502, General conditions to be met, Paragraph c, Limitation on manner of offering.

General rules and regulations promulgated under the Securities Exchange Act of 1934, Rule 10a-1, Short sales.

——, Manipulative and deceptive devices and contrivances, Rule 10b-21, Deception in connection with a seller's ability or intent to deliver securities on the date delivery is due.

——, Rules relating to over-the-counter markets, Rule 15c3-3, Customer protection—reserves and custody of securities.

Goldstein, Itay, and Alexander Guembel, "Manipulation and the Allocational Role of Prices," *Review of Economic Studies*, Vol. 75, 2008, pp. 133–164.

Harper, David, "Hedge Funds: Higher Returns or Just High Fees?" *Investopedia*, August 19, 2009. As of July 31, 2012: http://www.investopedia.com/articles/03/121003.asp#axzz22DPr5L4A

Harris, Lawrence, Ethan Namvar, and Blake Phillips, "Price Inflation and Wealth Transfer During the 2008 SEC Short-Sale Ban," June 18, 2009.

HedgeFund.net, undated web page. As of December 21, 2011: https://www.hedgefund.net/hfn_public/ marketing_index.aspx?template=aboutus.html

Hedge Fund Research, "Hedge Fund Industry Leverage Declines as Total Capital Reaches Record Level," press release, Chicago, Ill., May 17, 2011.

International Monetary Fund, *Global Financial Stability Report: Market Developments and Issues*, September 2003. As of July 30, 2012: http://www.imf.org/External/Pubs/FT/GFSR/2003/02/

Ivry, Bob, Bradley Keoun, and Phil Kuntz, "Secret Fed Loans Gave Banks $13 Billion Undisclosed to Congress," *Bloomberg*, November 27, 2011. As of July 12, 2012: http://www.bloomberg.com/news/2011-11-28/ secret-fed-loans-undisclosed-to-congress-gave-banks-13-billion-in-income.html

Kaswell, Stuart J., executive vice president and managing director, general counsel, Managed Funds Association, written statement for the hearing to review the implementation of Title VII of the Dodd-Frank Wall Street Reform and Consumer Protection Act, Part II, U.S. House of Representatives Committee on Agriculture Subcommittee on General Farm Commodities and Risk Management, February 15, 2011.

Keoun, Bradley, "Morgan Stanley Speculating to Brink of Collapse Got $107 Billion from Fed," *Bloomberg*, August 22, 2011. As of July 12, 2012: http://www.bloomberg.com/news/2011-08-22/ morgan-stanley-at-brink-of-collapse-got-107b-from-fed.html

Lattman, Peter, and Asam Ahmed, "Hedge Fund Billionaire Is Guilty of Insider Trading," *New York Times*, May 11, 2011. As of July 12, 2012: http://dealbook.nytimes.com/2011/05/11/rajaratnam-found-guilty/

Lewis, Michael, *The Big Short: Inside the Doomsday Machine*, New York: W. W. Norton and Company, 2010.

Lipsky, John, first deputy managing director, International Monetary Fund, "The Global Economy and Financial Markets: Where Next?" speech, c. 2007.

Litan, Robert E., "In Defense of Much, but Not All, Financial Innovation," Washington, D.C.: Brookings Institution, February 17, 2010. As of July 12, 2012: http://www.brookings.edu/research/papers/2010/02/17-financial-innovation-litan

Lo, Andrew W., *Hedge Funds, Systemic Risk, and the Financial Crisis of 2007–2008*, written testimony prepared for the U.S. House of Representatives Committee on Oversight and Government Reform, November 13, 2008.

Lynch, Sarah N., "U.S. Oil Speculative Data Released by Senator, Sparking Ire," Reuters, August 19, 2011. As of July 13, 2012: http://www.reuters.com/article/2011/08/19/ us-cftc-dataleak-idUSTRE77I4NR20110819

Mallaby, Sebastian, *More Money Than God,* Penguin Press, 2010.

Mallon, Bart, "Form PF," undated. As of October 5, 2011: http://www.hedgefundlawblog.com/form-pf.html

Managed Funds Association, "MFA Comments on Systemically Significant Institutions," letter to Timothy F. Geithner, Secretary of the Treasury, November 10, 2010.

————, "MFA Comments on Systemically Significant Institutions," letter to Timothy F. Geithner, Secretary of the Treasury, February 25, 2011.

McDonough, William J., president, Federal Reserve Bank of New York, statement before the U.S. House of Representatives Committee on Banking and Financial Services, October 1, 1998.

MFA—*See* Managed Funds Association.

"MF Global Holdings Ltd.," *New York Times*, updated June 5, 2012. As of July 30, 2012:
http://topics.nytimes.com/top/news/business/companies/mf-global-ltd/index.html

Misra, Vedant, Marco Lagi, and Yaneer Bar-Yam, "Evidence of Market Manipulation in the Financial Crisis," Cambridge, Mass.: New England Complex Systems Institute, December 13, 2011.

Oliver Wyman, *The Effects of Short-Selling Public Disclosure Regimes on Equity Markets: A Comparative Analysis of US and European Markets*, New York, 2010.

Paley, Amit R., and David S. Hilzenrath, "SEC Chair Defends His Restraint During Financial Crisis," *Washington Post,* December, 24, 2008.

Pástor, Lubos, and Robert F. Stambaugh, "Liquidity Risk and Expected Stock Returns," *Journal of Political Economy*, Vol. 111, No. 3, June 2003, pp. 642–685.

Pensions and Investments, "Largest Hedge Fund Managers," September 19, 2011. As of July 13, 2012:
http://www.pionline.com/article/20110919/PRINTSUB/110919925

Pozen, Robert C., *Too Big to Save? How to Fix the U.S. Financial System*, Hoboken, N.J.: Wiley, 2010.

Preqin, *2011 Preqin Global Investor Report: Hedge Funds*, London, undated.

President's Working Group on Financial Markets, *Hedge Funds, Leverage, and the Lessons of Long-Term Capital Management*, Washington, D.C., April 28, 1999.

PricewaterhouseCoopers, *Unfinished Business: Dodd-Frank—Entering Year Two*, New York, September 2011.

Public Law 63-43, Federal Reserve Act, December 23, 1913.

Public Law 73-291, Securities Exchange Act of 1934.

Public Law 91-598, Securities Investor Protection Act of 1970, December 30, 1970.

Public Law 111-203, Dodd-Frank Wall Street Reform and Consumer Protection Act, July 21, 2010. As of July 17, 2012:
http://www.gpo.gov/fdsys/pkg/PLAW-111publ203/html/PLAW-111publ203.htm

Public Law 112-106, Jumpstart Our Business Startups Act, April 5, 2012.

Regulation SHO, Rule 201, Price test.

Schapiro, Mary, chair, Securities and Exchange Commission, "The Road to Investor Confidence," Securities Industry and Financial Markets Association Annual Conference, New York, October 27, 2009. As of July 13, 2012:
http://www.sec.gov/news/speech/2009/spch102709mls.htm

SEC—*See* U.S. Securities and Exchange Commission.

Shadab, Houman, senior research fellow, Regulatory Studies Program, Mercatus Center, George Mason University, *Hedge Funds and the Financial Market*, testimony before the U.S. House of Representatives Committee on Oversight and Government Reform, November 13, 2008.

———, "Hedge Funds and the Financial Crisis," *Mercatus on Policy*, No. 34, Arlington, Va.: Mercatus Center, George Mason University, January 2009. As of July 13, 2012:
http://mercatus.org/publication/hedge-funds-and-financial-crisis

Standard and Poor's, "S&P 500," undated. As of July 30, 2012:
http://www.standardandpoors.com/indices/sp-500/en/
us/?indexId=spusa-500-usduf--p-us-l--

Stepleman, Robert, "Want to Beat the Market? Read this Column and Weep," *Herald-Tribune*, November 1, 2010. As of July 13, 2012:
http://www.heraldtribune.com/article/20101101/COLUMNIST/11011019

Strasburg, Jenny, and Amy Or, "Citadel Looks Set to Cut Bain on Investment-Banking Foray," *Wall Street Journal*, August 11, 2011.

Strasburg, Jenny, and Scott Patterson, "Behind Citadel's Bank Exits: Executive Departures Underscore the Challenges of Growth for Hedge-Fund Firm," *Wall Street Journal*, January 22, 2010.

"Strategy Focus Report: Securitized Credit," *HedgeFund.net*, April 11, 2011.

Strömqvist, Maria, "Hedge Funds and Financial Crisis," *Economic Review*, Vol. 1, January 2009, pp. 87–106.

Stulz, René M., "Hedge Funds: Past, Present, and Future," *Journal of Economic Perspectives*, Vol. 21, No. 2, Spring 2007, pp. 175–194.

"Tier 1 Capital Ratio, All U.S. Banks," *BankRegData.com*, undated. As of September 13, 2011:
http://www.bankregdata.com/allHMmet.asp?met=ONE

U.S. Code, Title 12, Banks and banking, Chapter 3, Federal reserve system, Subchapter X, Powers and duties of member banks, Section 371c-1, Restrictions on transactions with affiliates.

U.S. Commodities Futures Trading Commission and Securities and Exchange Commission, "Further Definition of 'Swap Dealer,' 'Security-Based Swap Dealer,' 'Major Swap Participant,' 'Major Security-Based Swap Participant' and 'Eligible Contract Participant,'" *Federal Register*, Vol. 75, No. 244, December 21, 2010, pp. 80174–80218. As of July 12, 2012:
https://www.federalregister.gov/articles/2010/12/21/2010-31130/further-definition-of-swap-dealer-security-based-swap-dealer-major-swap-participant-major

—————, "Further Definition of 'Swap,' 'Security-Based Swap,' and 'Security-Based Swap Agreement'; Mixed Swaps; Security-Based Swap Agreement Recordkeeping," c. 2011.

U.S. Department of Justice and Federal Trade Commission, *Horizontal Merger Guidelines*, issued April 2, 1992, revised April 8, 1997. As of July 12, 2012:
http://www.justice.gov/atr/public/guidelines/hmg.htm

U.S. General Accounting Office, *Long-Term Capital Management: Regulators Need to Focus Greater Attention on Systemic Risk*, Washington, D.C., GAO/GGD-00-3, October 1999.

U.S. Government Accountability Office, *Hedge Funds: Regulators and Market Participants Are Taking Steps to Strengthen Market Discipline, but Continued Attention Is Needed*, Washington, D.C., GAO-08-200, January 2008.

—————, *Private Fund Advisers: Although a Self-Regulatory Organization Could Supplement SEC Oversight, It Would Present Challenges and Trade-Offs*, Washington, D.C., GAO-11-623, July 2011.

U.S. Securities and Exchange Commission, "Form ADV," undated (a).

—————, "Form PF: Reporting Form for Investment Advisers to Private Funds and Certain Commodity Pool Operators and Commodity Trading Advisors," undated (b).

—————, *Implications of the Growth of Hedge Funds*, Washington, D.C., September 2003.

—————, "Securities and Exchange Commission," *Federal Register*, Vol. 72, No. 127, July 3, 2007, pp. 36348–36359.

—————, "Hedging Your Bets: A Heads Up on Hedge Funds and Funds of Hedge Funds," March 26, 2008a. As of July 31, 2012:
http://www.sec.gov/answers/hedge.htm

—————, "Invest Wisely: An Introduction to Mutual Funds," modified July 2, 2008b. As of July 13, 2012:
http://www.sec.gov/investor/pubs/inwsmf.htm

————, "'Naked' Short Selling Antifraud Rule," *Code of Federal Regulations*, Title 17, Part 240, September 17, 2008c.

————, "Amendments to Regulation SHO," *Code of Federal Regulations*, Title 17, Part 242, February 26, 2010a.

————, "Naked Short Sales," modified July 23, 2010b. As of July 13, 2012: http://www.sec.gov/answers/nakedshortsale.htm

————, "Exemptions for Advisers to Venture Capital Funds, Private Fund Advisers with Less Than $150 Million in Assets Under Management, and Foreign Private Advisers," *Code of Federal Regulations*, Title 17, Part 275, June 22, 2011a.

————, "Rules Implementing Amendments to the Investment Advisers Act of 1940," *Code of Federal Regulations*, Title 17, Parts 275 and 279, June 22, 2011b.

————, "Reporting by Investment Advisers to Private Funds and Certain Commodity Pool Operators and Commodity Trading Advisors on Form PF," modified January 5, 2012. As of July 13, 2012: http://www.sec.gov/rules/final/2012/ia-3308-secg.htm

U.S. Senate, *The Restoring American Financial Stability Act of 2010*, Conference Report 111-176, April 30, 2010.

U.S. Statutes, Title 48, Part 74, Securities Act of 1933, May 27, 1933.

Weiss, Miles, "Citadel, Millennium Above $115 Billion with Rule Change," Bloomberg, April 13, 2012. As of July 30, 2012: http://www.bloomberg.com/news/2012-04-13/ citadel-soars-to-115-billion-with-reporting-rule-change.html